ESTHER

ABINGDON OLD TESTAMENT COMMENTARIES

ESTHER

LINDA DAY

Abingdon Press
Nashville

ABINGDON OLD TESTAMENT COMMENTARIES
ESTHER

Copyright © 2005 by Abingdon Press

This book is printed on acid-free paper.

Library of Congress Cataloging-in-Publication Data

Day, Linda.
  Esther / Linda Day.
    p. cm.—(Abingdon Old Testament commentaries)
  Includes bibliographical references (p.).
  ISBN 0-687-49792-2 (binding: pbk. casebound : alk. paper)
  1. Bible. O.T. Esther—Criticism, interpretation, etc.   I. Title.   II. Series.

  BS1375.52.D39 2005
  222'.907—dc22

                2005012664

05 06 07 08 09 10 11 12 13 14—10 9 8 7 6 5 4 3 2 1

MANUFACTURED IN THE UNITED STATES OF AMERICA

CONTENTS

FOREWORD

The Abingdon Old Testament Commentaries are offered to the reader in hopes that they will aid in the study of Scripture and provoke a deeper understanding of the Bible in all its many facets. The texts of the Old Testament come out of a time, a language, and socio-historical and religious circumstances far different from the present. Yet Jewish and Christian communities have held to them as a sacred canon, significant for faith and life in each new time. Only as one engages these books in depth and with all the critical and intellectual faculties available to us, can the contemporary communities of faith and other interested readers continue to find them meaningful and instructive.

These volumes are designed and written to provide compact, critical commentaries on the books of the Old Testament for the use of theological students and pastors. It is hoped that they may be of service also to upper-level college or university students and to those responsible for teaching in congregational settings. In addition to providing basic information and insights into the Old Testament writings, these commentaries exemplify the tasks and procedures of careful interpretation.

The writers of the commentaries in this series come from a broad range of ecclesiastical affiliations, confessional stances, and educational backgrounds. They have experience as teachers and, in some instances, as pastors and preachers. In most cases, the authors are persons who have done significant research on the book that is their assignment. They take full account of the most important current scholarship and secondary literature, while not attempting to summarize that literature or to engage in technical academic debate. The fundamental concern of each volume is analysis and discussion of the literary, socio-historical, theological, and ethical dimensions of the biblical texts themselves.

The New Revised Standard Version of the Bible is the principal translation of reference for the series, though authors may draw upon other interpretations in their discussion. Each writer is attentive to the original Hebrew text in preparing the commentary. But the authors do not presuppose any knowledge of the biblical languages on the part of the reader. When some awareness of a grammatical, syntactical, or philological issue is necessary for an adequate understanding of a particular text, the issue is explained simply and concisely.

Each volume consists of four parts. An *introduction* looks at the book as a whole to identify *key issues* in the book, its *literary genre* and *structure,* the *occasion and situational context* of the book (including both social and historical contexts), and the *theological and ethical significance of the book.*

The *commentary* proper organizes the text by literary units and, insofar as is possible, divides the comment into three parts. The *literary analysis* serves to introduce the passage with particular attention to identification of the genre of speech or literature and the structure or outline of the literary unit under discussion. Here also, the author takes up significant stylistic features to help the reader understand the mode of communication and its impact on comprehension and reception of the text. The largest part of the comment is usually found in the *exegetical analysis,* which considers the leading concepts of the unit, the language of expression, and problematical words, phrases, and ideas in order to get at the aim or intent of the literary unit, as far as that can be uncovered. Attention is given here to particular historical and social situations of the writer(s) and reader(s) where that is discernible and relevant as well as to wider cultural (including religious) contexts. The analysis does not proceed phrase by phrase or verse by verse but deals with the various particulars in a way that keeps in view the overall structure and central focus of the passage and its relationship to the general line of thought or rhetorical argument of the book as a whole. The final section, *theological and ethical analysis,* seeks to identify and clarify the theological and ethical matters with which the unit deals or to which it points. Though not aimed primarily at contemporary issues of faith and life, this section should provide readers a basis for reflection on them.

Each volume also contains a select bibliography of works cited in the commentary as well as major commentaries and other important works available in English.

The fundamental aim of this series will have been attained if readers are assisted not only to understand more about the origins, character, and meaning of the Old Testament writings, but also to enter into their own informed and critical engagement with the texts themselves.

Patrick D. Miller
General Editor

ACKNOWLEDGMENTS

It has been my great pleasure to prepare this commentary on the book of Esther, one of the more continually intriguing works, in my opinion, of the biblical corpus. I am grateful to Patrick Miller and the editorial board for their gracious invitation to contribute to this fine emerging commentary series and for providing me a handy excuse to spend a few more enjoyable years immersed in Esther studies. Carol Newsom has my singular appreciation for her exceptionally careful and knowledgeable editing, her good-natured patience, and her helpful advice along the way. The help from my student assistant Jo Ramsey proved beneficial during the early stages of this project. I have been always gratified and often delighted by the kind efforts of librarians and colleagues in Pittsburgh who continually keep their eyes open for "Esther-abilia" of all sorts. Most useful also was grant assistance from the Catholic Biblical Association and the Wabash Center for Teaching and Learning. And the interest and energy of those with whom I have joined in conversation around the book of Esther, especially the students in my seminar courses and the women in the Bible study group at Third Presbyterian Church in Pittsburgh, have brought great joy.

INTRODUCTION

We live in a divided world. Groups wrestle with one another, vying for power, one faction at another's throats. Often these struggles fall along ethnic or religious lines, as in the Balkans, in Rwanda, in Northern Ireland, and in the Middle East. In the aftermath of the tragedy of September 11, 2001, many have become wary of those who look, dress, or worship differently. And we can never forget how we live in a post-Shoah world, with the greatest act of genocide in Western history only a few decades distant. The question of race relations is difficult and its complexities are not easily solved. On the one hand, tensions have escalated between peoples, yet on the other hand North American society has more individuals who do not fit neatly into any one ethnic category. In 2000, for the first time in its history, the United States census permitted individuals to indicate that they belong to more than one race. Furthermore, the position of women is especially problematic. Despite significant headway in equal opportunities for women, in business and religious institutions women still hit a glass ceiling, even if that glass is stained. Women belonging to a racial minority have an even greater question of identity, whether to find their primary community with other women or with other ethnic minority groups.

It is within this divided world that we read the book of Esther.

All interpretation is necessarily contextual. To state that a biblical book is "about" one particular thing is never a fully accurate assessment. Yet one important place where the book of Esther intersects with our current context is the issue of identity and minority survival. The story presents the situation of those who live as "other" within a dominant culture and the prejudice and persecution attendant upon such a situation. In essence, it is a story of ethnic conflict—the Persians against the Jews, the Jews having minority status in the Persian Empire. The conflict begins on a personal level, between two non-Persians of different ethnicities. Yet such prejudices do not remain on the level of the individual but become institutionalized. The various individuals and groups attempt to coexist in the same geographical space, yet, at least at first, with limited attempts to understand one another. A primary issue in the book is a functional one: minority survival. How does one survive when threatened as a person of a minority group? What should one do in a culture that is hostile to her very being? To what degree does one, as an individual in a larger society, permit his ethnic background to show? It is possible to see in the book a liberative element. The characters, especially Esther, exhibit attributes and actions of liberation, of protest against injustice and the struggle for emancipation (Craghan 1986; Costas 1988). Yet the passage to success is not without ethical concerns; violence pervades the "happy ending" of the story as the Jews respond to violence with violence. The book raises the questions of whether survival and success can come to one group only at cost to another and what constitutes fair play when one is faced with mortal danger.

The characters in the book, however, defy simple classification. Identities are not stable but shifting as individuals encompass multiple identities. It is not incidental that Esther herself, the main protagonist, is female. Exhibiting concerns of gender identity as well as ethnic identity, she is a woman in a man's world as well as a Jew in the Persians' world. Esther does not choose the same fashion as would a man to get her way but plays the power system to get to its top rung in the way that only an underdog could do. In this sense the book is important for feminist concerns and gender identity. Vashti and Esther are representative examples of strong women, but women who are forced to live their lives and to make their choices within the limits of a patriarchal system. The story's two queens represent differing strategies for maneuvering within an unsupportive, even hostile environment. The book of Esther raises the question of the adequacy of the models Esther and Vashti might provide for contemporary women who are also trying, in one way or another, to transcend their environment (Fuchs 1982; Wyler 1995; Mosala 1992). This is a particularly important concern when one is "other" in more than one way, as is Esther, the orphan/woman/Jew.

Though the book of Esther itself does not raise the issue of sexual identity, the work is relevant to the concerns of the homosexual community. In that Jewish identity can be concealed or revealed at the decision of the individual, it makes a particularly apt comparison with gay identity (Berman 2001; Sedgwick 1990, 67-90). At the beginning of the story, Esther, the hiding Jew, is analogous to the closeted gay; her decision to reveal her Jewishness is akin to a gay individual's decision to "come out" and involves similar risks. Such a public disclosure presents a challenge to what others assume that one is—Persian or straight. Esther's gradual revelation to her servants, then to Ahasuerus and Haman, and finally to the kingdom as a whole is the same process followed by homosexual individuals as they test the waters and develop increased self-esteem by coming out gradually to larger and larger communities. Acknowledging one's homosexuality or Jewishness follows the same process of restructuring one's self-concept and assimilating this new commitment with one's previous sense of identity. By the conclusion of the story Esther becomes a fully "outed" Jew.

Literary Aspects

Style and Structure

The book of Esther is written in a straightforward narrational style. Except for a few instances, the Hebrew is clear and understandable, despite the frequency of rare terms, but the simplicity of the book belies its consummate artistry. Aesthetically constructed, especially descriptive, and often elegant, the language can be understood as a type of "poetic prose" (Moore 1971, lv). The language tends, at times, to the verbose—not using one word when two (or three or four) will do just as well. Strings of synonymous terms, explanatory phrases, paired terms, and long listings of names occur frequently. Such linguistic details add to an overall sense of "officialese" (Levenson 1997, 11). Proportionately speaking, there is relatively little direct dialogue; most of the speech is reported indirectly by the narrative rather than quoted directly. Indeed, Mordecai, one of the primary characters, is heard only in a single statement (4:13-14). Consequentially, those instances when direct speech is provided tend to be especially significant: Memucan's and Haman's advising (1:15–2:4; 3:8-11), Esther's conversations with Mordecai (4:10-16) and with Ahasuerus (5:3-8; 7:2-10; 8:5-8; 9:12-13), and Zeresh's prescient replies to her husband (5:12-14; 6:13).

The pacing varies throughout the book, and, in general, considerable care is taken to indicate the times and durations of events (Noss 1993). The story begins at quite a leisurely pace, with several years elapsing between scenes (chapters 1–3), but quickens considerably as the events proceed (chapters 4–8). Especially surprising is the rapidity with which decisions carrying huge import upon the empire are made.

By means of thematic and semantic connections, the elements of the plot are carefully woven together into a seamless whole, and the work's skillful construction maintains the reader's suspense throughout. Frequent repetition of words, phrases, and entire sentences unifies the narrative. The book works as a whole, and, unlike many other biblical narratives, it is not easily or adequately divisible into discrete sections. Roughly speaking, chapters 1–3 serve as an introduction to all the main characters and to the problem of the situation, chapters 4–8 relate further complications and resolutions, and chapters 9–10 function as a fulfillment of the resolution with a view toward the future. Varying pivotal or climactic points have been proposed by interpreters of the book. Rather than isolating a single climax for the story, however, it is more accurate to recognize in its plot structure a series of defining moments. The first of these occurs at 4:15-16, when Esther makes up her mind to act. As she has experienced great success up to this point, the reader begins to anticipate that she will continue to prevail in this new endeavor. Another pivotal moment occurs at 6:11-13, with the visual prefiguration of Mordecai's rise in status and the aural prefiguration of Haman's fall in status. A final defining moment occurs at 9:1 when the narrative describes the final reversal of the story and makes fully explicit the Jews' ultimate victory.

Despite the book's concern with the serious issue of attempted genocide, the tone is humorous throughout. Much of the sense of the story is missed if one does not recognize how incongruous, and even funny, are many of its elements: the king of a vast empire who cannot make up his own mind, an advisor who is so afraid of one woman's autonomy that he legislates husbandly authority by imperial decree, a beauty treatment requiring a full year's time, and a beleaguered minority population being able to kill scores of thousands (cf. Jones 1977; Radday 1990). The plot progresses by means of a series of the unlikeliest and most improbable of events. Everything is exaggerated to the extreme. From the very first scene, the setting is drawn as an environment of total and complete excess—an excess of draperies, of drink, of servants, of virgins, of gallows, of death—in gigantic proportions. Irony of various types, both subtle and broad, pervades the story (Goldman 1990). For example, the disobedience of one queen is punished, but the disobedience of another queen is rewarded; the honor an egotistical man anticipates for himself falls upon another; and legislated patriarchy is simply ignored in the kingdom's households.

Characters

In the book of Esther, characters are revealed more through their actions than through narrative statements about them (either from the narrator or from other characters). Some of the characters act more as types, even as caricatures, than as full-fledged characters. Haman is the quintessential villain whose sole role in the story is opposition to others. The narrative reveals his inner thoughts more frequently than any of the other characters, but those thoughts always display a single trait—his egocentrism. Ahasuerus is an example of the "obtuse foreign ruler" type found throughout the Hebrew Bible, his incompetence parodied by the narrative (cf. Brenner 1994). The other characters manipulate him with ease. Vashti appears in one brief scene, portrayed solely as the woman with enough self-respect to refuse a degrading request (1:12). Mordecai's exterior is inscrutable. He is an enigma, both loyal and disloyal to the crown, a man who does not shy away from battle but who also displays concern for his young foster daughter. Esther, as is often noted, is the only character who approaches a rounded personality. More than one-dimensional, she is also the only character to change throughout the course of the story. First seen as a passive young girl, Esther matures into a shrewd and courageous individual who determines the future of an entire population. Finally, the reader must not overlook the participation of the servants, especially the eunuchs, who perform significant roles at several key places and (atypically for biblical literature) whose names are often provided by the narrative. Without the eunuchs' loyal services as attendants, advisors, secretaries, couriers, guards, and envoys, the plot could not move forward. (For extensive readings of the book's characters, see Fox 2001, 164-247.)

The naming of characters is significant, as five of the protagonists are regularly referred to by a single epithet that remains constant throughout the book. Vashti is most often cited as "Queen Vashti" until she loses the crown, after which she becomes simply "Vashti." Similarly, Ahasuerus is frequently named as "King Ahasuerus" or as simply "the king." These two individuals are important especially as holders of their political offices. Mordecai's name is often followed by the epithet "Jew" ("Mordecai the Jew"); in this way the most important aspect of his persona is his Jewishness. Haman's naming, similarly, highlights his antagonism towards those same people. He is repeatedly identified as "the Agagite" or as "the enemy of the Jews" and sometimes as both together. Esther is frequently identified as "Esther the queen"—a royal epithet that is more and more often added to her personal name as the story progresses and she increases in personal power and emotional maturity. Despite the fact that these last three characters have both ethnic and political identities that are significant to the story, never is Esther named by her ethnic Jewishness, nor are Mordecai and Haman named by their political positions.

The characters can be viewed in pairs that reflect both similarities and differences between them, "mirroring," in Brenner's terminology (1995, 74-75). Yet these doubled figures and paired alliances do not remain stable but shift along various lines. Esther and Mordecai pair off as Jews, but Esther and Ahasuerus pair off as royalty. Mordecai is not only like Esther in Jewishness, but also like Vashti in exhibiting blatant and unexplained disobedience, and like Ahasuerus in being a male with whom Esther learns how to negotiate. Esther mirrors Vashti and Mordecai mirrors Haman as the former and latter queen and prime minister, respectively. Esther, like Haman, is a foreigner in the Persian court, but she is also like Haman's wife, Zeresh, as they are two women who stand up against him. In such a manner, aspects of all these figures overlap, interweaving in multiple ways throughout the book. The characters develop different relationships among themselves, coming to the fore in new combinations as the plot progresses from scene to scene.

Moreover, all of the protagonists hide; they share a trait of not revealing their full identities. Esther, of course, hides her Jewish heritage from the Persian court. The story's final resolution occurs only when she chooses to reveal her full self. But the other characters are no less secretive. Mordecai conceals his reasons for not bowing, and Haman hides his personal contempt for Mordecai in evasive and impersonal rhetoric (3:8-9). Even Ahasuerus hides behind the wall of advisors who, *en masse*, make his policy for him. None of these figures permits herself or himself to be fully known by the others; all retain something of themselves from common knowledge.

Themes

The book of Esther exhibits several themes and motifs. None of them functions discretely, but all are interconnected and dependent upon the others. One such theme is power and space. Power is often materially conveyed through physical items—clothing, sceptre, throne, ring, palace furnishings, and the like. Generally speaking, the narrative tends to be physically descriptive; great care is taken to indicate the locations of events and the movements of the characters from one venue to another. Space does not function neutrally, but instead is key to the power structure in the Persian kingdom. In this environment, the king resides at the center, representing total political power. Power decreases proportionally as one moves away from this center, to the palace complex (including the women's quarters), to the king's gate, to the citadel, and finally out to all the provinces. Physically coming closer to the center increases one's power, and everyone in this story comes into the king. One can note the frequency that the Hebrew term *lipnê,* "to the presence of," appears with Ahasuerus as its object. Esther first travels to the women's quarters, then to the king's bedroom, and then to throne room with her requests; Haman goes into Ahasuerus's presence with his plan; and finally Mordecai, with Esther, goes before the king to gain authority to author an edict. All the characters gain their power by physically moving from the margins to the center. In contrast, Vashti's attempt to keep power *away* from the king, to keep it in her own space, backfires.

Shifts in power (empowerment and disempowerment) tend to occur at parties (Berg 1979, 31-35). The book of Esther contains a series of ten parties, culminating with the celebration of Purim, a party *par excellence.* The Jews' two fasts also act as an auxiliary counterpart within this theme, concerned also with drink and food, but in abstention. The Hebrew term used to indicate these events is *mišteh,* typically rendered in the NRSV as "banquet." Of the forty-six occurrences of *mišteh* in the Hebrew Bible, a full twenty of them are found in the book of Esther; the book clearly stands out in the canon in terms of the level of attention it grants to partying. The Hebrew verb from which the noun derives can signify either generally drinking any sort of liquid or specifically drinking alcohol, much as the English verb "to drink" does. Similarly, *mišteh* can signify a general feast, including food (for instance, Gen 19:3; Job 1:5; Isa 25:6). However, in numerous places throughout the Bible it clearly indicates an event focused exclusively upon drinking alcohol and the resulting inebriation, a drinking party of some sort, perhaps similar to a modern-day cocktail party (1 Sam 25:36; 2 Sam 13:27; Isa 5:11; Jer 51:39; also possibly Gen 29:22). The term is clearly used in the latter way in the book of Esther, for at the many places that references to these social events occur, the story never refers to food or to the act of eating. Knowing that the characters are under the influence of alcohol during this continual partying helps the reader understand more clearly why they act as irrationally as they do.

Power is promulgated in the kingdom through writing, though this same writing is also a sign of the kingdom's bureaucracy. Words are not merely spoken but must be written down—then written again and again in multiple languages (1:22; 3:12; 8:10). Vashti's deposal is written into Persian law (1:19), Mordecai and Esther's act of saving the king is recorded in the official annals (2:23; 6:1-2), and a series of several letters is written and sent throughout the land (Haman's edict, Mordecai's edict, and Purim legislation). In these written documents, persons and concepts are both written in, or inscribed (a new queen, a new holiday), and written out, or exscribed (Vashti, the Jews, the Persian wives) (Beal 1997, 83-84). In the story, writing lends validity, stability, and permanence; in this sense it is a social function. Yet the permanence that is sought in this land of the unalterable written decree does not, in the end, hold. In various ways the story's documents serve to undermine the very authority and stability they ostensibly attempt to uphold—others author the king's letters, written decrees are undone, and official annals remain useless unless, only by chance, they happen to be read (cf. Bal 1991; Clines 1990, 48-51; Fewell 1992, 11-17).

This prevalence of the written decree highlights the book's emphasis upon law. The Hebrew term *dāt* "edict," which is rare in the rest of the Hebrew Bible, appears with great frequency in the book of Esther. Signifying a radically different sense from the biblical *tôrâ*, or "instruction," *dāt* indicates an official decree issued by the government for its citizens. Decrees are given to be obeyed, and obedience (along with its corollary, disobedience) functions as a theme in the story. How an individual chooses to respond to the royal law or to commands from other people drives the progression of events and their outcomes. Some characters, at some times, opt for obedience: Esther willingly enters into the selection process and obeys Mordecai about not revealing her ethnic identity while doing so; Mordecai obeys Esther in initiating the three-day fast; the Jews obey Esther and Mordecai's legislation about the new Purim holiday. Yet at other times these same individuals choose disobedience. Mordecai disobeys the royal command to bow to Haman, and Esther disobeys the royal institution that forbids a person's coming before the king at her own inclination. And, of course, Vashti's blunt disobedience to Ahasuerus's request for her presence begins the entire sequence. At the story's conclusion, two decrees, which are in essential conflict with each other, exist, forcing the Persian citizens, Jew and non-Jew alike, to decide which of them they will obey. Illustrated by the various characters' decisions regarding the many royal decrees throughout the story, the book ultimately raises the question of civil disobedience, of choosing to take a stance according to conscience, despite possible, even probable, negative consequences.

Honor, along with its counterpart shame, pervades the story (for fuller explication, see Klein 1995; Laniak 1998). Through the situations and concerns of its characters, the book of Esther reflects shame and honor codes in ancient society. Haman is the most vocally concerned for his personal honor (5:11-13; 6:6, 12), yet he is twice visibly shamed through chaperoning Mordecai's parade and through death by public hanging. Likewise, Ahasuerus honors himself by throwing the most lavish of parties. Mordecai's honor is upheld by his fine Jewish heritage (2:5-6), but this same honor is affronted by Haman's demands. His honor is later made public as he travels the streets in the king's attire and is promoted to the highest office. The Jews' shame, indicated by their sackcloth, turns to honor with their ultimate triumph. Gender concerns also play into this theme. Not only do honorable and shameful activities vary, depending upon gender, but also Vashti's actions serve as public shaming for Ahasuerus, to which he responds by attempting to legislate universal male honor and female shame (both for Vashti and for all wives). Esther gives honor to her foster father through her unquestioning obedience and succeeds with the king by presenting her petition in a way that, in contrast to Vashti, does not shame him.

Reversals are another significant element of the book. The phrase *wĕnahăpôk hu'*, "but it was overturned," at 9:1 acts as an interpretive key to the entire proceedings (Levenson 1997, 8; cf. also Fox 2001, 158-63). The plot flows not in a logical and linear progression, but with loops and switchbacks. The reader is led to expect a certain result, but—surprise!—its opposite occurs instead. Not only the fate of the main protagonist, the orphan who becomes queen, but also the fortunes of others are part of this "Cinderella story." Though Mordecai disobeys authority just as Vashti does, he does not receive the similar punishment one would expect. Zeresh's advice shifts from pro-Haman to pro-Mordecai in a few short hours. The Jews' grief turns into joy. Mordecai gains Haman's job and possessions, along with guardianship of the king's ring; his decree overturns Haman's decree, word for word; and Haman hangs on the stake intended for Mordecai. These theses and their antitheses are often linked by similar or repeated vocabulary, and they lend a sense of symmetry to the book as a whole.

Genre

One issue in Esther scholarship on which there is little agreement is that of the book's genre. Whereas it is not necessary to recount all the various suggestions that have been proposed through the years (note the excellent summaries in Bush 1996, 297-309, and Fox 2001, 141-52), this very variety is in itself illustrative. The book of Esther exhibits aspects of a diversity of types of biblical and ancient literature, and in this sense it is representative, to greater and lesser extents, of such various generic categories. The book incorporates the morphological structures and the types of characters of folklore, featuring classic elements such as the upright and righteous hero, the fair maiden, the stupid king, the treacherous counselor, and the loyal servant, all within a luxurious setting (Niditch 1987, 126-45). It also retains aspects of a court legend, with its setting in a foreign court and its emphasis upon a competition between the courtiers Mordecai and Haman

(Wills 1990, 153-91). Although an identification of the book as a historicized wisdom tale draws too tight a connection between Esther and biblical wisdom literature (Proverbs, Job, and Qoheleth), the book certainly includes wisdom concerns, including its contrast between wise (as represented by Esther) and foolish (as represented by Haman, Vashti, and even Mordecai) choices, along with other features characteristic of wisdom literature, such as a remote deity and a lack of interest in the Jerusalem cult (Talmon 1963; also White 1989 and Brenner 1998). Its emphasis upon the establishment and celebration of Purim reveals its character as a festival etiology, explaining the origin of the Jewish festival (Bush 1996, 300, 306). The book also represents the genres of literary carnivalesque, farce, and burlesque, with its low comedy, parodies, exaggerations, somatic concerns, and ludicrous effects (Craig 1995; Berlin 2001a, xvi-xxii).

All of these various genres are reflected in the book of Esther. In general, however, the book of Esther can best be classified as an example of the genre of Jewish novel (Wills 1995, 1-39, 93-131). Jewish novels (such as Daniel, Judith, Tobit, and Joseph and Aseneth) present contexts, structures, situations, and characters that are more developed than biblical short stories (such as Ruth and Jonah). The story of Esther is similar to these contemporaneous Jewish diaspora works (cf. Day 1998). It, along with these other Jewish novels, lies between oral and written culture, an example of the popular literature that was being created for an increasingly literate citizenry. This "novelistic impulse" continued in the production of the Greek versions of the story, which reflect to a greater degree than does the Hebrew version the emerging Greek novel form (Day 1995, 214-32).

ORIGINAL CONTEXT

The book of Esther reflects the situation of the diaspora, and one of the reasons it was produced was certainly to address the needs of the Jewish community living outside of Palestine. The story is set after the exile (2:6) and is part of the postexilic period of Israelite history, when many Jews were living away from their homeland of Judah. As is often observed, there is no concern for items and ideas that feature prominently in other Israelite literature: land promised to the ancestors, the Jerusalem cult, Torah observation, or an autonomous Israelite state under a divinely appointed monarch. Unlike the roughly contemporaneous works of Ezra and Nehemiah, the book of Esther does not suggest that the goal of proper Jewish living is to return to Judah; instead, it promotes the idea that Jews can live personally fulfilling, and even socially successful, lives in exile from Palestine. It addresses a post-exilic crisis of identity: who are we, if we not only do not live in Judah, but also do not even want to? In this way the Esther story resembles other biblical stories concerned with diaspora living (the Joseph stories, Daniel, Tobit, and Jonah). Among these, the book of Esther expresses acceptance of holding dual loyalties, loyalty both to Judaism and to the foreign state (Greenstein 1987, 234). The message is that when living in a foreign environment, one need not totally separate from the dominant culture but become involved in it. With such involvement, it is possible even to become politically well placed and economically prosperous in foreign society. Furthermore, from the foreign perspective, Jews are shown to be not detrimental to that regime but beneficial to it. The story provides an example, especially in the figure of Esther, of how Jews can succeed: rather than standing against a foreign system, they should choose to work within it (White 1989; Humphreys 1973). Yet the story also reflects the unpredictability that postexilic Jews experienced as a minority culture, constantly in a position of vulnerability. Individual Jews need to rely upon all their inner resources in the diaspora, for the responsibility falls upon them, and not the state, to ensure Jewish continuity (Fox 2001, 148; Berlin 2001a, xxxiv). In such a way the book of Esther functioned to address Jews in the Second Temple period.

From the textual evidence, it indeed appears as though the story was found useful by various ancient Jewish communities. Though the focus of this commentary will only be upon the Hebrew version, two other primary versions of the story exist, both in Greek. These Greek versions vary from the Hebrew version in two significant ways. First, both Greek versions contain six segments of material that are not included in the Hebrew version (traditionally designated as the "Additions"), segments which present prayers of Mordecai and Esther, an altered scene of Esther's approach before Ahasuerus, verbatim texts of Haman's and Mordecai's edicts, and a dream and its interpretation at the beginning and the end of the story. Though the edicts seem to have been originally composed in Greek, the rest of this material appears to have been translated from a Semitic (either Hebrew or Aramaic) original. Second, in one of these Greek versions (the A, or Alpha, text), the details and presentation of the story vary significantly from the Hebrew version, so much so that it probably represents a different tradition of the story altogether. (For discussions of the intriguing relationships among these three versions and hypotheses about their developmental history, see Clines 1984a; Fox 1991; Day 1995; Dorothy 1997; Jobes 1996; De Troyer 2000.) The possible presence of a court legend in the library of the ancient Qumran community also suggests the prevalence of these types of stories and their circulation and adoption during the Hellenistic period (Talmon 1995; Crawford 1996). For the concerns of the historical context of the book, all of this evidence makes clear that the story of Esther along with others like it were popular in their day. They were adapted and readapted by ancient communities, presumably to meet the needs of new generations.

The setting of the book is the Persian Empire, with most of the action occurring in the city of Susa. Susa served as the administrative capital of the empire and the winter residence of the king, and inscriptional evidence portrays its fortified acropolis as constructed of costly imported building materials. Ahasuerus, the king in the book, is commonly thought to reflect the Persian king Xerxes I, who reigned 486–465 B.C.E. Our knowledge of Persian political history is dependent to a great extent upon ancient Greek authors. Many of the details and attitudes in the book of Esther are similar to those attributed to the Persian Empire by these Greek historians: for example, the geographical extent of the empire, the seven-member advisory council, the equine postal system, and the keeping of official diaries. In this sense, the book reflects a typical conventional view of Persia (Berlin 2001a, xxviii-xxxiv). The book also uses both Persian names and Persian-sounding names for its characters (Horbury 1991; Yamauchi 1992). But elements that do not fit with this portrayal of the Persian Empire are also included; for example, Persian queens were allowed to come from one of only seven noble families, the name of Xerxes' queen was Amestris, the number of provinces was twenty, and the concept of unalterable laws is unknown. (Discussions of aspects of the book that are and are not histori-cally probable can be found in Moore 1971, xxxiv-xlv; Clines 1984b, 256-63; Fox 2001, 131-37.) The book of Esther is clearly, in modern terms, a work of fiction. The author placed her or his story against a Persian background, incorporating elements of what was currently understood about Persian royal life.

With regard to social conditions, there is some evidence to sug-gest that the ethnic relationships presented in the story may reflect actual conditions in the Persian Empire. It is, admittedly, particu-larly difficult to reconstruct social attitudes and relationships in ancient times. The Persian Empire, especially in the earlier stages of its history, was widely presented as benevolent toward the vari-eties of people within its borders. The Persian political adminis-tration showed significant degrees of tolerance toward the local languages, laws, customs, and religious practices found within its diverse population; and ethnic groups seem to have enjoyed a degree of autonomy not experienced under other ancient regimes. For instance, historical documents reveal that, at various times in Persian history, there was ethnic diversity among workers at building sites, the army represented the diversity of the empire as its ethnic contingents maintained their own leadership and weapons, a royal autobiography was translated into all the local languages, and an indigenous Babylonian governor was promoted to the position of satrap in the royal administration. The story of Esther reflects these sorts of ethnic tolerances, of beneficial rela-tions among peoples and support for ethnic autonomy from the royal administration. Religious tolerance was also Persian policy, as local cults and temples were supported by new Persian leaders. When a Jewish temple in Egypt was destroyed by local authorities, for instance, the matter was taken to the Persian satrap, who ordered that it be rebuilt. In the story of Esther there is similar official tolerance, as the Jews Mordecai and Esther are supported by the king and allowed to attain high positions in the Persian royal administration. Antisemitism, like that displayed by Haman, is, therefore, not part of the ethos of the Persian period in ancient Near Eastern history, but is a later historical phenomenon.

Because of its interest in diaspora living, the provenance of the book of Esther is almost certainly not Palestine but elsewhere in the Jewish diaspora, though it could come from anywhere throughout the region. Composition in the east may be slightly more likely because of its Persian setting, but not significantly more probable. The dating of the book, however, is more difficult. Its language reflects a later period in the development of the Hebrew language (late biblical Hebrew), and includes Aramaic and Persian loanwords, which would signify a postexilic date (Bergey 1984, 1988). If Ahasuerus does indeed reflect Xerxes I, the very earliest time of composition would be the mid-fifth century B.C.E. The latest possible time is determined by a colophon concluding the Vaticanus Greek version that indicates how the translation was brought to Egypt during the reign of Ptolemy and Cleopatra, which, depending upon what rulers are meant, would be either 114/113 or 78/77 B.C.E. These endpoints produce a broad span of up to four centuries, but narrowing down the time of composition more precisely within the Persian and Hellenistic periods is not a task that permits much certainty. Arguing that the book's pro-Gentile attitude precludes composition during the Hasmonean period, most interpreters generally date the book to the fourth or third century B.C.E. and do not attempt to identify a more specific time. Some scholars, however, find composition during the Persian period to be more likely because of the generally favorable attitude displayed toward the Persian political hierarchy (Clines 1984b, 272) or due to the similarities with Greek historiographical literature during that time (Berlin 2001a, xli; Berlin 2001b). Other scholars place the time of composition later on this spectrum, in the Hellenistic period, because earlier persons would have readily recognized the book's historical inaccuracies (Fox 2001, 139), because of the severity of the Jews' revenge and simi-

16

larities to other Greek fictional literature (Wills 1995, 110), or because the story could likely have been used to promote Queen Shelamzion and other women in political leadership (Ilan 1999, 133-37). The book's clear similarities with attitudes about Persia expressed in Greek historiography should not preclude a date in the Hellenistic period. Such writings could certainly still be in circulation at that time, their attitudes still influencing authors.

THEOLOGICAL CONCERNS

A perennial question about the book of Esther is whether it even *has* theological concerns. After all, God is neither active nor mentioned in the story. The Greek versions address this issue simply, by writing God into the events as an active participant and by characterizing Esther and Mordecai as pious individuals. But in the Hebrew version, not only is there no mention of the deity, but also there are no elements that suggest a religious concern (prayers, Torah observance, temple worship, and the like). The reader most likely would not be troubled about such an absence if this story had not been placed in the biblical canon, surrounded by literature that concerns itself with things religious. Despite the absence of the divine name, however, many scholars do find the book of Esther to reflect the presence of God. God is viewed as a character in the story, "though one who evidently prefers to remain anonymous" (Bechtel 2002, 14); all the events are "sustained by a powerful, yet, hidden, 'force'" (Beller 1997, 2) and "the God who appears hidden nonetheless remains present" (Berg 1979, 184). The places where the deity is often caught lurking backstage, peering through the curtain, are Mordecai's and Zeresh's references to the Jews' survival, the Jews' fasting, and all the happy coincidences and reversals of fortune. Moreover, some scholars also argue that reading the book within its canonical context renders it as one more chapter in Israel's salvation history, or *Heilsgeschichte* (Berg 1979, 182-83; LaCocque 1987). Yet whether one finds in the story an active deity or not, an active humanity is certainly present. Action begins with people, not with God, and the book places high emphasis upon human initiative, responsibility, and accountability. Whether God is perceived to be present or not, what *is* clear is that human beings are called to oppose the evil they see around them.

The absence of God in the book of Esther is not, in actuality, its problem, but its benefit. Not to be explained away, the book's theological ambiguity is indeed the point. The book of Esther is a story of uncertainties. Is God involved, or is it chance that is running the show (Besser 1969)? It is impossible to know for sure. The book of Esther reflects the very human situation of looking back at a situation that has turned out well and asking, "Did God do that?" but never being able to know for certain one way or the other. One interpreter's "go[ing] back and forth" on the issue of a secular or religious character to the story indicates a proper readerly response to its inherent ambiguity (Fox 2001, 244). The book presents an accurate view of the typical human situation, a recognition that most people's experience is not like that of the biblical patriarchs and prophets to whom God speaks directly. It reflects the fact that God cannot often be seen clearly, and it is impossible from a human perspective to know whether God is present but hiding or is completely absent. The book of Esther does not attempt to convert skepticism into faith but permits actions to remain in their theological ambiguity.

Though the book of Esther is not religious, it is exceptionally *biblical*. Other parts of the biblical canon are echoed in it, and the story is patterned after these earlier stories to greater and lesser degrees. The biblical work with which the book exhibits the closest connection is the Joseph story in Genesis 37–50 (Berg 1979, 123-65). The situational context of both is similar: set in a foreign court, the characters rise from humble origins to attain high political positions, which provide them the means to help their people in a crisis. There are also structural similarities between the two works, and the book of Esther repeats certain linguistic expressions from the earlier story. Though mentioned a few times, God is likewise not very present or active in Joseph's situation. The book of Esther also reflects the exodus from Egypt. The figure of Esther parallels the figure of Moses, in that she likewise delivers the Hebrews/Jews from a foreign people bent on their destruction and an annual holiday is initiated to commemorate the deliverance. The ancestries assigned to Mordecai and to Haman link the book with 1 Samuel 15, which tells of a battle between Saul and Agag, the king of the Amalekites. Their enmity is thus read against an ancient ethnic rivalry, and the Jews' abstention from taking plunder may act as a corrective to the earlier story, in which Saul is instructed by God not to take plunder after the victory but chooses to disregard that command. Like Daniel 1–6, the book of Esther is set in the opulent court of eastern (Babylonian and Persian) kings, its characters have both Hebrew and non-Hebrew names and are promoted to higher and higher administrative positions, and their enemies in the court are executed in punishment. Though it is an extra-biblical work, the widely popular book of Ahiqar bears certain similarities to the Esther story, particularly to the figure of Mordecai, and was expressly used in the composition of the book of Tobit (Tob 1:21-22; 2:10; 11:18; 14:10). Ahiqar resembles Mordecai as an administrative official who adopts and instructs his nephew and is threatened by a royal officer but saved from death when another is executed in his stead. The books of Ruth and Judith exhibit similar circumstances of women being forced to find their way in a male environment and similar methods of accomplishing their objectives (carefully laying traps for male leaders that include taking advantage of men's drunkenness, using their sexuality as a tool, and succeeding through initiative and cunning).

In sum, the echoes of all of these works in the book of Esther manifest the strong intertextuality between it and rest of the biblical tradition. This story connects these Jews in Persia with the larger story of Israel; it finds a place for the displaced. Yet it continues this larger story not from the point of view of *ʾereṣ yiśrāʾēl*, the land of Israel, but instead from the point of view of the exiled community (Berlin 2001a, xxxvi). All of these echoes of earlier literature would most likely have been recognized by the book's earliest readers. In this sense the book places itself squarely within the scriptural tradition, if not within a strictly theological tradition.

Rather than expressing clear theological assertions, the book of Esther instead prescribes an action: throw a party. On its surface level the book proposes as its purpose an explanation of how the festival of Purim came into being. Purim is presented more in the sense of a national holiday, akin to the United States' Independence Day or Thanksgiving, than a religious celebration. As the sole festival in the Jewish calendar that is not commanded in the Torah, the book seeks to legitimize this new holiday. Celebration of Purim, however, actually appears to have preceded the composition of the book. The link to Haman's casting of *pûr* (3:7) gives the sense of a fabricated etymological explanation (not unlike others frequently seen throughout the Hebrew Bible) to present a reason to celebrate a holiday of that name that was already in existence, and the legislation about two different days of celebration (9:17-19) probably reflects the fact that the holiday was currently being observed in different places on different days. Scholars have attempted to determine, though without much certainty, the origins of this festival as possibly a Babylonian or Persian new year's festival (Moore 1971, xlvi-xlix; Polish 1999).

With regard to ethnic relationships, two details about Purim are of particular significance. First, historically the Jews apparently adopted a foreign holiday and adapted it for their own use, and second, in the story this holiday is established in an especially Persian way (a law is written and disseminated throughout the land). Both of these aspects demonstrate a merging of cultures, an interrelationship between Jews and non-Jews. In the book of Esther, Purim is presented as a celebration not of a military victory, not of the violent defeat of thousands, but instead as a celebration of the time of rest that follows that victory. With great joy, the people are to celebrate their release from danger. In this way Purim is to serve as hope for the absence of persecution and prejudice for future generations as well as remembrance of past deliverance from a mortal threat. One aspect of the book's presentation of Purim that is not often noted but is essential for ethical concerns is its encouragement of generosity. Jews are charged not only to rejoice but also to observe charity, to give to the poor (9:22). The purpose for the holiday is ultimately not self-serving but community-serving. Such care for the poor of society is often enjoined elsewhere in the Hebrew Bible, especially in Deuteronomy (e.g., Deut 15:1-11; 24:14-15) and the prophetic literature (e.g., Amos 2:6;

8:4-6; Ezek 18:12). The observance of Purim stipulates that Jews of successive generations are to behave like Esther, to help others who are oppressed by their circumstances just as she helps her people in their oppression.

It is imperative to remember that we read the book of Esther after the Shoah (more commonly but less appropriately called the Holocaust). It is often stated that after this atrocity in human history, all theology must be completely reconsidered. This necessity is most especially the case for interpretation of the Esther story, for it comes far too eerily close to the events of the Shoah. Though Western history is replete with discriminations of various sorts against the Jewish people, the Shoah reflects the desire for their complete and total annihilation. As in the story, Jews were not defined in religious but in ethnic terms; a matter of ancestry rather than belief designated one as Jewish. Therefore, reading the book of Esther in a post-Shoah world means that its horrors reside not on the story level, but are real and experienced; it is no longer possible to treat it only as a fiction, a tale of a long-ago time in a faraway place. Moreover, those in the Christian tradition must acknowledge the antisemitism that has frequently been a part of Christian interpretation of this biblical text throughout the past several centuries. Far too many Christian interpreters have read this story as a statement about Jewish nationalism, treating the story's violence as normative and essential to Judaism rather than as a defensive response to mortal danger (for fuller discussions of the antisemitic nature of much earlier interpretation, see Fox 2001, 212-34; Greenstein 1987, 225-26; Fackenheim 1990, 87-92; Beal 1997, 4-12).

With the Shoah, the book of Esther no longer resides on the outskirts of the biblical canon but has moved to its center. We have seen Haman, "the enemy of the Jews," in Adolph Hitler, the enemy of the Jews. These two autocrats' commands were the same: "to destroy, to kill, and to annihilate all Jews, young and old, women and children" (3:13). Yet one must exhibit care when making such comparisons, for the biblical Haman is not successful in his attempt at genocide, but his real-world counterpart was frighteningly successful, exterminating one-third of the worldwide Jewish population. In the story, the fortunate Esther and Mordecai save the Jews; in the Shoah, thousands of nameless Esthers and Mordecais risked their own lives for Jews—but there was no such luck for most of them (Fackenheim 1990, 62). Theological meaning, therefore, must not only be seen in terms of ultimate victory, but also be found at a different level, at the level of human resistance. Redemption is to be found not only in the ultimate saving of lives but also in the very act of resistance to evil (Raphael 2003, 12-13; Sweeney 1998, 157-60). The book of Esther represents the responsibility of individuals to come forward when encountering evil, to act to the best of their ability to prevent evil from running its course. Such human action is especially necessary when God seems absent. Jewish theology speaks of the *hester panim* (most prominently discussed in post-Shoah theology by Berkovits 1973). The *hester panim* of God signifies, literally, the "hiding of the face" of God, reflecting God's absence, or turning away, in certain situations. In times of divine invisibility—such as the Shoah, such as Haman's edict—it falls upon human beings to counter evil. In times of such atrocities, perhaps human resistance is the proper—indeed the only possible—response.

COMMENTARY

AHASUERUS'S ROYAL PARTIES (1:1-8)

The book of Esther commences by describing two parties: one for public officials and one for the general populace, both thrown by the king, Ahasuerus. These are the first of a progression of drinking parties occurring throughout the book of Esther. Ahasuerus first throws a party for the palace officials and employees (vv. 2-4). Immediately upon its completion, he gives another party, grander in scope but shorter in duration, this one in the royal garden's courtyard (vv. 5-8). Details of time, place (for the second), guest list, and duration are observed by the narrative.

Literary Analysis

The function of this episode is introductory. In a basic sense, the description of these two parties gets the plot moving: the parties provide the opening for the significant events concerning the queen in the following section. This section also gives the reader an impression of what the palace environment is like. As most of the action of the book transpires within the palace walls, such information is necessary for proper understanding of the story's events. It also functions as a foretaste of things to come, an introduction to certain of the main themes that will be found throughout the rest of the story: partying, royal pomp and appearance, being in the presence of the king, and obedience.

This section serves, furthermore, as an introduction to the character of King Ahasuerus. On the one hand, one sees the generosity of this monarch. He gives parties in the grandest style, sparing nothing for his guests. On the other hand, this generosity has a purpose and a price, for Ahasuerus's design in having so many people come to the palace is to elicit their admiration, that they might see "the great wealth of his kingdom and the splendor and pomp of his majesty" (v. 4). Ahasuerus wants to show off. Materialism and power are important to this king, and, moreover, that his officials recognize this power and wealth. One might compare King Ahasuerus's concerns with the model of kingliness put forward in other parts of the Hebrew Bible; his concern is not at all with the wisdom, just sovereignty, piety, and compassion a ruler is to embody and by which a ruler is to be evaluated (cf., e.g., Deut 17:14-20; Pss 72, 101; 2 Sam 23:3-4). One might also note that this is a fairly young king; he has been ruling only some two-odd years (v. 3). Perhaps his desire to impress others through a display of wealth is a sign of his immaturity. As this story progresses, this inexperience will become even more evident as Ahasuerus feels the need to rely greatly upon the advice of his counselors and advisors.

The first of the many decrees of the king that occur throughout the story is mentioned here. At the second drinking party, the guests literally imbibe at Ahasuerus's demand: "The drinking was in accordance with the decree, without restraint" (author's translation) and "the king had given orders to all the officials of his palace" (v. 8). The characters' actions of trying to impose their will upon others propels the plot here and elsewhere (Fox 2001, 17). This description may reflect the Greek historian Herodotus's account of the practice of guests at Persian banquets having to drink whenever the king drank. More likely, however, it reflects Ahasuerus's intent that people drink as much (or as little) as they desire. This remark sets the tone of permissiveness that will run throughout the subsequent events.

Exegetical Analysis

Social position is clearly important from the very beginning of this story; the Persian Empire is revealed as based upon a system of political hierarchy, as is evident through this pairing of parties. The first party is for members of the palace system who are officially affiliated with the king, literally, "his officials and his servants." The terminology may reflect different categories of individuals, greater and lesser officers of the king. If so, the second party mirrors similar social categories; "both great and small" are invited, but now from among the general population of the citadel. Those residing outside of the citadel receive no celebration at all. The duration of the drinking parties is vastly different, an incredible half a year, "one hundred eighty days in all," for the royal employees but a mere seven days for the general population. Though the location of the first party is not mentioned (perhaps it is in the palace, a place with which the royal officials would be familiar), the general population is not permitted in the palace but kept outside in its garden court. Already King Ahasuerus demonstrates a certain egalitarianism, in inviting both the lowest and the highest of each category to his drinking parties. Yet segregation within Persian society, indicated here by those with and without access to the king, is also clear.

The theme of royalty is likewise introduced in this initial episode. The "citadel" (vv. 2, 5) probably indicates the high place in the center of the city of Susa, the royal part of the capital city where the palace complex is located, separate from the general city (cf. 3:15; 4:1; 8:15). Not only do the events take place in a royal setting, in the palace, but the very authority of King Ahasuerus is stressed. The point of the drinking parties is so that he can show off "the great wealth of his kingdom and the splendor and pomp of his majesty" (v. 4). The prevalence of the term *malkût,* here and throughout the story, especially indicates this theme. *Malkût,* which occurs thrice in this section, signifies something to do with royalty. Here it refers to the royal throne (v. 2), to the royal wine served at the second drinking party (v. 7), and to royal power (v. 4). Elsewhere in the book, the term *malkût* denotes a royal position of authority or power (1:19 [the second occurrence]; 4:14; 5:1), the political or geographical domain (1:14, 20; 2:3; 3:6, 8; 9:30), the royal house or palace (1:9; 2:16), the royal crown (1:11; 2:17), royal clothing (6:8; 8:15), and a royal edict (1:19 [the first occurrence]). The effect of these numerous references to aspects of royalty, initiated in this section, is to render an impression of exceptional political power and influence.

Verses 6-8 are especially noteworthy. The second drinking party is described in some detail, in far greater detail than is typical of biblical narrative, which tends to be laconic in its depictions of physical surroundings. Verse 6 consists of a series of descriptive terms in quick succession. In the Hebrew text, the verse begins immediately with the description of the white hangings (the NRSV's "There were ...," beginning the sentence, is added). The nobles of Persian society would have been accustomed to the palace appointments and would not note the physical surroundings in such great detail. Rather, the recounting in these verses gives the impression of coming from the point of view of one of the "small" ones of verse 5, who is experiencing the royal palace area for the very first time and is overwhelmed by its opulence. Not being able to contain her or his awe, this one lists breathlessly and excitedly item after item that she or he sees, in rapid succession, hardly pausing for breath. And the perspective is notably a domestic one; it is the décor (household furnishings) and the dinnerware that are noted instead of, for example, the architectural or engineering aspects of the palace complex that would have been similarly awe-inspiring.

Verse 6 contains numerous rare words for which it is difficult to ascertain exact meanings. Four of the terms occur only here in the Hebrew Bible (*karpas*, "cotton curtains"; *bahaṭ*, "porphyry"; *dar*, "mother-of-pearl"; *sōḥāret*, "colored stones,"), one appears only here and another place in the book of Esther (*ḥûr*, "white [fabric],"), and four others are used only a few times in the Hebrew Bible (*bûṣ*, "fine linen"; *gālîlîm*, "rings"; *šēš*, marble" or alabaster; *riṣpâ*, "mosaic pavement"). Though scholars may not know precisely to what each Hebrew term refers, the overall impression is an overwhelming sense of great luxury and beauty. Visually thematic, the colors are a preponderance of reddish-purple and white: the white cotton, the fine linen that is probably white byssus, the marble or alabaster stone, and the mother-of-pearl, in combination with the violet hangings (*tĕkēlet*, translated in the NRSV as "blue"), the purple cords, the porphyry (a purplish or reddish stone), and the (presumably red) wine (v. 7).

This description provides overtones both of the Jerusalem temple and of international trade. Two of the terms in verse 6 are frequently used elsewhere in the Hebrew Bible, particularly in the priestly tradition, to refer to fine fabrics used in temple hangings (*tĕkēlet,* "violet hangings"; *'argāmān,* "purple"). These terms, along with "fine linen" *(bûs),* are also used, particularly in the prophets, to refer to textiles acquired in commercial transactions from other places in the ancient Near East. Both of these aspects together function in particular ways. They provide a sense of how cosmopolitan Ahasuerus's kingdom is, having items from all over the known world, which prefigures how the palace administration will show itself to welcome persons from various places and cultures. The narrator of the story can also be seen as wanting to portray Ahasuerus's environment in religious language, his palace as a temple. From the point of view of the Israelites in diaspora who are living in Susa and attending the second drinking party, the religious overtones of this terminology would bring home to them quite clearly the loss of the temple, reminding them that they are living in a place where the glories of the temple are replaced instead by only the glories of state. The international overtones, moreover, would give those Israelites the visceral sense of being in a foreign place, now that they see those exotic items of which they had previously only heard. The choice of terminology in this verse also prefigures the exaltation of Mordecai later in the book. Three of the same terms (*hûr,* "white [fabric]"; *bûs,* "fine linen"; and *'argāmān,* "purple") are used to describe Mordecai's fine raiment after he has been promoted by King Ahasuerus and Queen Esther (8:15).

Theological and Ethical Analysis

This introduction sets up a story world without God. What is revered and obeyed is the state, not God or priests or Torah. The physical is what is presented as important in this environment, not the spiritual; personal wealth, not personal piety. Earthly happiness rather than eternal happiness is the ideal. Such a this-worldly approach is reminiscent of the book of Qoheleth's admonition to eat, drink, and be merry in the face of life's enigmas (Qoh

2:24-26; 3:12-15; 5:18-20; 9:7-8). In this world, it is government, not religion, that has the greatest effect upon the lives of the people. In modern terminology, one might say that the Persian Empire represents not just a separation of church and state, but an environment in which there is no "church." In a certain sense, King Ahasuerus's debauchery might be read as demonstrating the dangers of such a "godless" society.

One cannot help but question the sense of responsibility represented in the figure of Ahasuerus. He appears as an individual with a compromised code of ethics and a questionable moral fiber, at least with regard to his regnal duties. For six months he has all the province governors and the army residing in Susa. Whereas his celebration is most likely a holiday welcomed by his invitees, it leaves the entire empire without administrative support and military defense for an entire half year. Who knows what needs might arise out in the provinces while their leadership is partying several hundred miles away? By this act, Ahasuerus demonstrates a certain disregard for the Persian population at large.

The king's actions represent a display of ostentatious wealth. He himself overindulges. In addition, he tries to impress others with money and gifts, choosing, in effect, to buy their affection, respect, and loyalty rather than to gain their respect through being a good ruler. A life of wealth and power seems to be what is important to Ahasuerus—or at least that is the picture he outwardly presents to the world. The reader does not see into any inner life that the king might have; it is all surface, for outward show (cf. Levenson 1997, 45-47). Far from the values presented by the Persian ruling class are the prophetic admonitions against wealth and its misuse (e.g., Amos 4:1-3; 6:1-8; Isa 2–3; 28:1-4). The beginning of the book of Esther presents a picture of conspicuous consumption, at least for the ruling class. Any society in which wealth leads to consumerism and "keeping up with the Joneses," the acquisition of expensive items for the mere sake of having them and showing them off to others, might see itself in this portrayal of the Persian court and its ruler.

Yet one should not judge the actions of this inexperienced king too harshly. On the one hand, the reader cannot help but wonder how many of the poor could have been fed with the money used to throw these two parties. On the other hand, however, the royal actions represent a recognition of the importance of beauty in life. This episode presents a certain ambiguity; it can be read as a picture either of excess or of abundance (Bechtel 2002, 21). With his second party, Ahasuerus gives to the common folk in the citadel more elegance than they would see in their everyday lives, bringing beauty into the lives of those who might not typically encounter it. Furthermore, with his generosity he creates an atmosphere of abundance for subjects who otherwise would not experience such bounty—even if it lasts only for the seven days of the royal party. As the Persian subjects appear to be regularly taxed (2:18; 10:1), the administration's activities represent the dilemma faced by every political administration when determining how to disburse its treasury. For what should taxpayer money be spent? How does a government adjudicate among the competing needs of its peoples? One might argue that a society needs to support the fine arts, that beauty possesses the intangible benefit of enriching the lives of those who experience it. Though the parties serve to bolster the ego of the king, in so doing they also bring joy to the people.

Vashti's Refusal (1:9–2:4)

The focus in this episode begins with Vashti, as she throws yet a third drinking party, this one specifically for women (1:9). Her refusal to cooperate when Ahasuerus requests her presence at his party initiates the problem that the remainder of this episode will resolve. The royal advisors suggest solutions to which the king agrees, and they are executed throughout the kingdom.

Literary Analysis

Most of the action is seen from Ahasuerus's perspective, starting from his decision to send the seven eunuchs for Vashti (1:10-12). The setting shifts at 1:13 to center upon Ahasuerus's conversation with the advisors. A great amount of narrative space is awarded to a direct quotation of Memucan's counsel (1:16-20), and later of the attendants' counsel (2:2-4). Indeed, these are the only instances of direct speech that the reader hears; the queen's and the king's statements are only recorded indirectly (1:10, 12, 13, 22; 2:4; 1:15 also more likely reflects the reported, not the direct, question of Ahasuerus). The narrative exhibits a fine example of satire through Memucan's speech, which represents the situation in disproportion to its actuality. Ahasuerus's recognition of the need for a new queen is a separate scene (2:1-4), but it is not clear how much time elapses between the sending of the edict about Vashti's banishment and women's subservience (1:21-22) and his subsequent recollection about Vashti (2:1).

Vashti, though a key player, is not heard throughout this entire episode. The narrative reports merely that "Queen Vashti refused to come at the king's command conveyed by the eunuchs" (1:12). Nor is any explanation given as to *why* Vashti does not come at her husband's request, though interpreters have surmised a variety of possibilities: she is to wear only her crown and nothing else (according to the Megillah and the Targums), only concubines are to attend men's parties (according to Greek beliefs about Persian customs), or her dignity will not permit her to parade herself before drunken men. A further possibility is that perhaps she is too occupied with the duties of hosting her own party and simply does not wish to desert her guests. As understanding Vashti's motivation is quite a large gap for the reader to fill—one might argue that it is essential to understanding this character—it is curious why the author chose not to reveal her thoughts. Thus Queen Vashti slips into and out from this story quickly and quietly; this is the first and only instance where she is involved. By the end of this episode she is exscribed, literally written out of the story (Beal 1997, 25). Yet Vashti's presence continues to echo throughout the subsequent events. As one of the two female characters in the book, she functions as a foil, a comparative figure to Esther, the second queen. The narrative explicitly makes this comparison at 2:17, and through the remainder of the story one cannot adequately evaluate Esther's choices apart from Vashti's choice.

The events in this episode begin a progression of movement from Susa to the provinces. News of Vashti's action is the first pronouncement that goes out in this story, as 1:17 anticipates how "the matter of the queen will go forth to all the women" (author's translation). The second missive is the letter that Memucan proposes (1:19). These two occurrences begin a steady stream of communications that travel from the palace to the countryside: Haman's decree (3:12-15), Mordecai's counter decree (8:9-14), and Esther and Mordecai's legislation about Purim (9:20, 30).

Exegetical Analysis

Vashti's drinking party (1:9) may be compared to the king's two drinking parties. In sum, the reader knows much less about Vashti's party than about the others. There is no similar description of the exact location (cf. 1:5), the environment (cf. 1:6), the libations (cf. 1:7-8), the duration (cf. 1:4, 5), or the purpose (cf. 1:4). The guests are merely noted as "the women"; the narrative does not report their social rank or where they reside, unlike the guests hosted at the previous two events (cf. 1:3, 5). The reason for the brevity of description is not clear. Is Vashti not as eager to show off with fine appointments and beverages as her husband? Or, because this party is merely for women, does the narrator consider it to warrant less explication? That only women are invited to this drinking party now invites reconsideration of who might have been the guests at the second party. The narrative relates how King Ahasuerus invites all "the people" in the citadel of Susa (1:5). As the Hebrew term ʿam, "people," includes all people generally, of both genders, the reader might have expected both women and men of the city to be guests at that drinking party. Now, however, exclusively women are included at Queen Vashti's party. The reader, therefore, is now drawn to question whether only men were involved in the king's second drinking party, the women being left for the queen's affair, or whether the women are given another party just for them. In other words, are the women recipients of gender discrimination, not invited to the king's party, or are they given special treatment, invited both to the king's party and to the queen's special party just for them? Most interpreters of the story argue that women would not likely have dined with men at such events in ancient Persian society (Moore 1971, 13; Fox 2001, 18, 20; Levenson 1997, 46; Berlin 2001a, 11-13; Beal 1999, 8; Bechtel 2002, 23; Clines 1984b, 278). Yet, as the narrative is ambiguous, there is no obligatory reason to assume women's absence at Ahasuerus's week-long drinking party. As women also tend to look with interest upon other women's beauty (otherwise modern women's magazines would have no reason to sport photos of beautiful models on their covers month after month), female party guests could certainly be expected to be among Vashti's admirers (1:11). The narrative also makes no distinction as to their rank, as it does with the general populace earlier, the "great and small" (1:5); it gives the impression that it makes no difference whether noble or common women are involved and that the social status of these women is immaterial.

Verse 10 presents the first vision of an inebriated King Ahasuerus, a state he will maintain throughout much of the story. The notation "when the king was merry with wine," literally "when the heart of the king was good with wine," unquestionably indicates that he is drunk. This same language is used to refer to other individuals' drunken conditions following royal feasts (for example, Nabal [1 Sam 25:36] and Amnon [2 Sam 13:28]), and to Qoheleth's advice to enjoy one's food and drink (Qoh 9:7). As with other biblical feasts that result in drunkenness, this one will likewise upset social relations by its conclusion (Walsh 2000). This phrase is a clue to Ahasuerus's character. His hasty and unreflective actions exhibited throughout the story reflect his lack of sobriety after participating in all the drinking parties. In this scene, Ahasuerus still wants to show off his power, as was his goal for the first party (1:4). This time, however, the alcohol causes him to do so in an inappropriate manner.

The king's request to Queen Vashti is a clear case of voyeurism; he desires to parade his wife in front of party guests who are quite probably as drunk as is he after all their revelry (1:11). That it requires seven servants to convey one woman is another touch of the overblown nature of this story, akin to the party that lasts half a year (1:4). The guests of both of King Ahasuerus's drinking par-

32

ties now appear to be joined togetl
"the people" from the second party
cials" from the first party (1:3). Wh
especially Queen Vashti's beauty, but
come wearing "the royal crown." Th
elements suggests that Vashti's beauty
but augmented by her political powei
men in high positions of political or
power is an aphrodisiac: it makes he
attractive. However, a gender difference
royal aspect ("the throne of his royalty,'   malkûtô) is associated primarily with his political power, his wealth of possessions
and of territory (1:1-4), whereas Vashti's royal aspect ("a crown of
royalty," *keter malkût*) is associated primarily with her physical
beauty (author's translations). One might question exactly what
this phrase, "the royal crown," signifies. Does it suggest Vashti's
own autonomous political authority, or does it instead suggest possession, like "the royal wine" (*yên malkût*; 1:7) that the king is also
presenting to his guests? Noting what happens to Queen Vashti, in
that she is treated like the king's possession, might imply the latter.

That King Ahasuerus is an individual of great passion is
revealed at 1:12. At Vashti's refusal he becomes instantly angry;
the repeated expressions "the king was enraged" and "his anger
burned within him" emphasize the intensity of his emotions. Here
the effect that his abundant drinking has had upon him becomes
evident; instead of thinking logically, he reacts in haste and with
his emotions only. This scene sets the stage for his later display,
during another drinking party, of instant and fierce anger at
Haman (7:7). The same Hebrew term, *hămātô*, "his anger," is also
used there and linguistically links the king's responses. The emotion of anger plays a key role in the story, so much so that Segal
finds anger to be the key to the book's plot structure (1989). Here
Ahasuerus first shows himself to be uncomfortable when things
are not going smoothly. Along with not liking to be disobeyed, he
dislikes chaos and uncertainty; wanting people (here, his party
guests) to be pleased, he hastens to return the situations to a
happy equilibrium.

ther characteristic of the king is revealed: he prefers
decisions for himself, but rather to have others make
him. Here he requests advice from his palace advisors.
gh initially it may seem good strategy that Ahasuerus repeat-
ly abdicates matters to the wise ones, the "sages," it ultimately
reinforces the impression that he is a foolish, and not a wise, ruler.
The terminology describing these individuals is unusual. Literally,
they are introduced as "the wise ones who knew the times, . . . who
knew law and judgment." The second phrase is parallel to the first
and further explicates it; that is, those who know law and judgment are the ones who therefore know the times and who are
knowledgeable about both legal and traditional Persian customs
(Crawford 1999, 882). As with the seven eunuchs earlier (1:10), it
is atypical of biblical literature to provide the names of servants,
especially when they have no direct acting or speaking roles (compare, for instance, the seven unnamed advisors in Ezra 7:14). The
explicit mention and nomenclature of these fourteen persons in all
gives an impression, perhaps even a humorous impression, of the
large entourage always surrounding the royal personages. Though
King Ahasuerus asks his question of all seven advisors, only one—
Memucan—responds. That it is his idea alone, and not the joint
collaboration of all the sages, is clear at 1:21, when Ahasuerus does
as Memucan (alone) has proposed. The other six appear
to be there only for show, just as the queen is expected to be—
present but silent. They are allowed to agree (1:21) but not to influence. It is becoming clear that this administration functions not
upon collaboration, but upon authoritarianism. Just as the plan of
one man (Haman) will ruin things for an entire group of people
(the Jews in Persia), here the plan of another sole man (Memucan)
ruins things for another group of people (the Persian women).

Ahasuerus inquires of his advisors what should be done
"according to the law" (1:15). Memucan, however, does not
answer the question from a legal standpoint. One would expect
that he would cite from a preexisting legal collection, or at least
refer to a legal precedent. Instead, Memucan gives the impression
of making up something on the spot. He acts not as legal counsel
who knows laws and customs (1:13), but as one who takes on the

authority to *make* laws and new customs. The manner in which
Memucan presents his answer blows the response out of propor-
tion to the deed. He begins by saying, "Not against the king alone
has Queen Vashti acted subversively, but against all the leaders
and all the peoples who are in all the provinces of King
Ahasuerus" (author's translation). What Ahasuerus sees as a "sin
of omission" (1:15), Memucan represents as an action that is actually insurgent (Beal 1999, 12-13). Though Vashti's action could,
in one sense, be seen primarily as a personal infraction (i.e.,
against the king alone), Memucan's rhetoric presents the case as
one of national import, a crisis of state, resulting in "no end of
contempt and wrath" (1:18). In his presentation, he treats Vashti's
beauty not as her personal possession, but as belonging to everyone. He continues to exaggerate the situation. Memucan imagines
the Persian women speaking out not only against their own husbands, as Vashti had done, but against "all the king's officials"
(the NRSV does not translate the "all," *kōl;* 1:18). In so doing, he
actually grants a great degree of influence to the queen; she is presented as so powerful that, by mere example, she can affect every
household to the furthest reaches of the empire. It is a subversive
thought indeed, in this system of male hierarchy, that one woman
would be influential enough to cause such a ruckus. The suggested punishment of banishment likewise fits the overblown
atmosphere of this scene and of the book as a whole (1:19).
Ironically, the effect of such a widespread pronouncement will
bring far more attention to Ahasuerus's shaming than if it were
left only to the tongue-wagging of the party guests (Fox 2001, 24).

Memucan is unable to disguise the fact that he is speaking not
out of concern for the empire, but instead out of his own personal fears. He first presents the situation in terms of "all women"
(1:17). As he continues to hypothesize the ensuing scenario, however, he reveals his true concern, limiting his imaginings to the
upper class, "the noble ladies" speaking against "the king's officials" (*śārê hammelek;* 1:18). Recently described as a Persian
"official" himself (*śārê hammelek;* 1:14), Memucan shows himself
to be actually worried about peace in his (and his colleagues') own
households, not peace in the kingdom. The upshot is that "all

women" (1:20) must pay for his own personal fear. As Haman will do later, Memucan speaks out of his own self-interest; he enacts kingdom-wide legislation, affecting "high and low alike" (1:20), to solve a personal problem.

The final phrase of 1:18, "and there will be no end of contempt and wrath," is ambiguous with regard to the subject of these two emotions. Most likely, however, Memucan anticipates the "contempt" to be the same as he, in the previous sentence, imagines from the ladies (1:17), and the "wrath" as that of their husbands in response. This male anger directly reflects Ahasuerus's wrath (1:12). By playing out the king's wrath on the empire as a whole, Memucan insinuates that all husbands share the same characteristics as those of Ahasuerus, in making unreasonable demands upon their wives and then responding in great anger if they disobey. By anticipating that they will respond as intemperately as a spoiled and foolish king, Memucan gives little credit to the general populace.

In this episode, hierarchical structures are upheld. The narrative is careful to situate clearly the societal rank of the officials; they are the ones who "sat first in the kingdom" (1:14). Memucan also employs significant terminology when speaking of marital situations. Rather than using the more general Hebrew term ʾîš, which means either "man" or "husband," he chooses the term baʿal (1:17, 20). Baʿal can be used to refer to one's husband as well, but its principal meaning is "owner," "lord," or "ruler." Memucan, by the choice of this more specialized term, is reminding the men that they are the ones in charge, that they are lords and masters, and their property (that is, their wives) is not obeying. It is important to him to stress the hierarchical nature of the married couples. But even though the man is the ruler in the marriage, their class is not alike, for Memucan is as careful to note their same "high and low" rank (1:20) as the narrator was of the party guests (1:5). The statements referring to the future queen are likewise hierarchical in nature. The next queen will be "better than" Vashti (1:19), superior to her in what one might expect to be essential ways. Criteria for determining what makes for a better queen are not explicitly spelled out, this vagueness possibly the strategy of a good courtier who allows flexibility for the king to understand the statement however he chooses (Moore 1971, 11). One might decipher from the forthcoming process that such a woman would be more beautiful, more pleasing to the king, and more obedient in her willingness to be prepared and then brought before him for the scrutiny that Vashti eschews (2:2-4).

The theme of honor is used in this scene, particularly in terms of women's attitudes toward their men. In 1:17, women are anticipated, literally, to "demean" their husbands. Memucan's fear is not that women will hate their husbands, but instead that they will look down upon their men and therefore cause them to be looked down upon by others. The essence of Queen Vashti's action, therefore, is interpreted in terms of honor and shame, her refusal to come at the king's command as shaming the king. The antidote for such behavior is to "give honor" to one's husband (1:20). The basic meaning of this Hebrew term yĕqār, which is used frequently in the book of Esther (cf. 1:4; 6:3, 6 [twice], 7, 9 [twice], 11; 8:16), is "to be precious, be appraised, be costly." Women are, therefore, literally expected to assign value to their husbands. In his speech, Memucan confuses physical obedience with giving honor. In trying to legislate respect, which is something that must be earned, he is not recognizing that actions do not necessarily reflect the heart. Haman will later make the same mistake in attempting to legislate obedience when what he also really desires is honor and respect (3:1-6).

In this episode, speech and the act of speaking are emphasized. Ahasuerus's request of Vashti is referred to as a "word" (1:15), and the influence of Vashti's action is also referred to as a "word" of the queen (1:17). Then the women of the kingdom, who hear Queen Vashti's utterance, are expected to "speak" to their husbands in response (1:18). The government will send out a "royal word" (1:19), and 1:21 refers twice to Memucan's speech ("the word" and "according to the word of Memucan"). There is, therefore, a chain of influence through speech: Ahasuerus's speech causes Vashti's speech, which causes the Persian women's speech, which causes Memucan's speech, which ultimately causes official government speech. Furthermore, this section initiates another significant progression that runs throughout the book. The term *ma'ămar,* "word," used here in 1:15, appears later for Mordecai's word of advice to Esther (2:20) and for Esther's word about Purim to all the Jews of the kingdom (9:32). This terminology elucidates a theme of the story that commences in this scene: first Ahasuerus acts as a commanding figure, then Mordecai does, and then ultimately Esther herself does.

In King Ahasuerus's response to Memucan's suggestion (1:21-22), the king does not exactly follow the advice of his courtier, despite the narrator's optimistic comment that "the king did just as Memucan proposed." Though Memucan had suggested that the ruling should be about Vashti and her successor ("that Vashti is never again to come before King Ahasuerus; and let the king give her royal position to another who is better than she;" 1:19), the king actually writes about what each *man* should do, with no mention of queens, present or future, at all. What the king does choose to ordain is hierarchy in the home, for "every man [to] be master in his own house." The verb "to be master" *(śārar)* is related to the nouns used at 1:3, 1:14, and 1:18 to refer, respectively, to the palace officials, the seven nobles closest to the king, and the royal ladies of the kingdom. In essence, this law is ordaining that now each common man can be a noble, a king in his own castle—all that he need do is keep his wife in line.

The final phrase, "and speak according to the language of his people," is a rather odd statement within the context of this scene, so unexpected that some translations, including the NRSV, choose not to include it. All told, it renders the king's missive as quite an inclusive statement. The letters are all in the local dialects, so that all the people can understand them without difficulty. Their message is further inclusive, in asserting that every man has the right to converse in his native tongue. The imagery of written ("in its own script") and oral ("in its own language," literally "its own tongue") transmission may further assure that literacy will not be a barrier to the message getting through; both those who understand by reading and those who understand by hearing will be accommodated. This decree is an example of how the Persian Empire is portrayed as accommodating of peoples of all ethnicities.

As chapter 2 commences, the king begins to look forward. The introductory statement "after these things" *(haddĕbārîm)* can literally mean "after these words." This term acts as a double entendre, to be understood as referring generally to all the events that have transpired, but also, in its basic meaning, echoing all the speaking and writing of chapter 1. Following Memucan's long speech and the letters in all the many various languages, this is after many words indeed! (Chapter 3 begins in the very same fashion, there referring to the "words" recorded in the royal annals.) The narrative now reports that Ahasuerus becomes no longer angry and then remembers Vashti. It is odd, in a way, that he recalls her *after* he loses his rage. As his anger had been so linked with the queen and her actions, one might instead expect that when that anger diminished so would his concern about her. Or, in thinking of Vashti, is he really merely recognizing that she is no longer around and therefore he should have a new queen? Ahasuerus's reflections progress through three stages (2:1). First, "he remembered Vashti"; second, he recalls "what she had done"; and third, he remembers, literally, "how she had been cut off" (author's translation). This progression of Ahasuerus's memory replicates the threefold progression of Vashti's action: first, her introduction; second, her refusal to attend the drinking party; and third, the men's decision against her. The reader can note how Ahasuerus absolves himself of any responsibility. He appears to suffer from amnesia with regard to what he himself did to bring about the present queenless situation, thinking solely of what Vashti did, as though her actions were autonomous and not precipitated by his own. For instance, he could have recalled that he banished her, but instead chooses to think in the passive mode, "she had been cut off." In his mind, Ahasuerus considers his hands to be clean in the whole matter.

Regarding those who are sought to replace Vashti, the king's servants suggest three primary qualities: they must be young, they must be virgins (or, more specifically, of marriageable age, as the Hebrew term *bĕtûlâ* denotes), and they must be beautiful (2:2-3). Age, sexuality, and appearance are what matter in the selection process, at least as it is initially formulated. It is not surprising that beauty is desired, in that this was a valued characteristic of the previous queen (1:11). Perhaps, in searching for young women the desire is to secure a new queen who is inexperienced in the world, shy and insecure, who would not disobey and disrupt the Persian patriarchy the way that Vashti did, nor even think in her pretty young head to do so. The government, however, is apparently open to a queen from a non-Persian cultural background, for the servants suggest that the search be commenced "in all provinces" of the kingdom (2:3). As this is the very same "all provinces" to which the king's letter, in a variety of languages, was sent, the new queen might not even speak Persian (1:22). This second plan is as overblown as the first; as Vashti's actions are anticipated to affect all women (1:17), now all young women will be affected (2:3) (Beal 1999, 22). One might also question the effect of this search upon the families, and especially the parents, of these young women, who will lose their daughters for a king's whim. Might Ahasuerus not find a way to secure a new queen without interruption to so many families in the kingdom? This decision appears especially ironic, following as it does upon Memucan's speech about upholding familial harmony throughout the kingdom (1:17-18).

The concluding verse of this section reiterates a theme that has been building throughout, that of the king's pleasure. This episode presents an inclusio with regard to Ahasuerus's emotions: he began happily in good spirits (1:10), then became distressed (1:12), and now finally he is happy again (1:21; 2:4). Moreover, those around him have been actively attempting to please him all along. Memucan, in suggesting a solution to Vashti's refusal, shows himself an able courtier as he couches his suggestion in language desiring what is "pleasing" to King Ahasuerus (1:19). Likewise the servants, suggesting a procedure to select a new queen, are careful to stress the king's pleasure as the deciding factor (2:4). It will become evident as the story progresses that this is a king who likes to be pleased, and those who are successful in getting the king to do as they wish are those who are able to please him.

In the end, what can one conclude about Vashti? What has she done? It is not one of the official Persian edicts *(dāt)*, so prevalent throughout the story, that she is accused of violating. The "word" of Ahasuerus that she does not follow does not carry the same official status (1:12, 15, 17); it is only a personal command. Therefore, the language suggests less that Vashti is guilty of transgressing a law of the kingdom than disagreeing in a personal matter, of going against the king's desires. Yet the resulting legislation is made far more official than a personal grievance, being written among the official royal edicts (1:19). On the one hand, one might wonder whether justice is served in this instance, whether the punishment fits the crime. On the other hand, might not Vashti be pleased with the ruling? She does not want to come before the king at his party. Her punishment is not banishment from the palace, nor execution, but "that [she] is never again to come before King Ahasuerus" (1:19). Though the narrative provides the reader no explicit comment regarding Vashti's desires or emotions, one might speculate that she is getting exactly what she wants—not to have to come before the king and, more broadly, no longer to have to play all the political games of queenship.

Theological and Ethical Analysis

On both the individual and the corporate levels, the episode paints a somewhat troubling picture. Ahasuerus does not act in ways that subjects might wish of their monarch and, in general, demonstrates emotional immaturity. His is the reaction of an individual who has much, but still throws a tantrum when faced with something he cannot have. He is under the illusion that his wealth and power grant him privilege. As van Wijk-Bos aptly notes, "A man with too much money, too much time, too much power is thwarted in his desire for total control. Ahasuerus is like a peacock who cannot get enough of having others admire his display" (1998, 111). Corporately, the reader is presented with an overblown bureaucracy, one in which it takes seven people to do the job of one, yet the end result seems no better despite the six additional persons on the payroll. The environment of excess, therefore, continues. The moral values of this society seem askew, as the well-being of one segment of society (the women—both the wives and the young women) is sacrificed to provide for the happiness of another segment (the men—the husbands and the king).

Memucan represents the government official who puts his own needs and fears above the needs of others. The episode provides a caution against the human propensity to desire public honor. The only way that these individuals can see to build themselves up is by putting someone else down, as Haman will also do later in the story. Yet they try to achieve honor by decree rather than through honorable action. True honor, however, cannot be commanded. In general, one sees how corruption by the few at the top of a society inevitably makes life more difficult for the many at the bottom.

In addition, the patriarchal nature of this society is made abundantly clear. Men are the acting subjects, gaining their power by means of the objectification of women. Women are presented as male property, possessions who are not valued for their character but for their beauty, their sexuality, and (in the case of the prospects for the new queen) their youth. The degree of their worthiness is the degree to which women are able to, or choose to, please men. Not considered acceptable for their own sake and on their own terms, female worth is measured instead by male assessment, adjudicated in the eyes of a man. Fragile male egos abound and are expected to be propped up by the womenfolk of the land. Yet there appears to be little opportunity for true communication between the sexes in this society; women and men are presented as working against one another more than cooperating with one another. First was the physical separation, as the women were given a separate, possibly less luxurious, party; and now is Memucan's suggestion of antagonism between wives and husbands. Memucan's assumptions hearken back to the image given in the biblical creation story's original conception of the difficult relationships that will exist between female and male partners (Gen 3:16). The proposed result of forced hierarchy hardly seems a satisfactory solution in the long run.

The abuses of position, wealth, and gender in this environment, however, do not remain unacknowledged, but are critiqued by the queen's action of resistance. In the face of such an unjust society, Vashti can be seen as a countercultural figure. She is the individual who "just says no" to society's expectation and evaluation of her. She is a strong-willed character with an independent bent, and her courage is admirable. And if Vashti indeed does not follow the king's request because she deems it degrading, she appears principled and forthright. Vashti can be viewed as a model for others who would follow their conscience, no matter what the cost. Not willing to be an object of Ahasuerus's action, in her refusal she maintains herself as a subject of her own action, and in so doing she opposes abusive power structures. Her action is, in that sense, prophetic. It is for these reasons that the figure of Vashti is often viewed positively in light of liberation theologies, most especially feminist theology (Gendler 1976; Laffey 1998, 213-15; Bankson 1985, 39-53), but also gay liberation theology (Comstock, 49-60). Some may argue that Vashti's is an unwise choice, that the accommodating Esther opts for the more pragmatic and ultimately more effective response. Yet in certain situations persons need to stand up against what they perceive to be immoral or unjust, to speak for righteousness without regard for the consequences. Freedom can prove to be expensive. But there are moments in life when enduring enslavement, in whatever guise it presents itself, is no longer an option, and one becomes willing to pay that price. At such turning points, one can only maintain personal integrity by standing up and taking the risk.

ESTHER BECOMES QUEEN (2:5-20)

Esther's rise to queenship is depicted in this episode. Along with the rest of the kingdom's eligible young women, this Jewish orphan is taken to the palace and undergoes preparation to meet King Ahasuerus, as her guardian Mordecai watches from afar. The king esteems Esther over all the others and throws a grand coronation party in her honor.

Literary Analysis

The episode continues 2:1-4 and exhibits certain thematic and vocabulary connections with that previous scene. The overall narrative sequence, however, is interrupted twice. The first interruption occurs in verses 5-7, which consist of a rather lengthy introduction to Mordecai and his cousin and foster daughter, Esther. Though Mordecai is introduced first, he is really only a secondary character. The focus immediately shifts to Esther, and she is the protagonist highlighted throughout this episode. Only in verse 8 does the sequence resume from 2:4, when the newly introduced Esther takes her place along with all the other young women being herded up for the king and experiences palace life. The second interruption to the narrative flow comes in verses 12-14, which amplify 2:3*b*-4*a* by illustrating in greater detail the general procedure of the selection process. Focus returns to Esther again, as her own night with the king and the results from it are described (vv. 15-18). The episode concludes as it begins, with another reference to Mordecai and Esther's dependence upon him (vv. 19-20).

The episode exhibits both delay and speed in the timing of its events. When Ahasuerus finally chooses his new queen, he is in the seventh year of his reign (v. 16), four years later than the date when the story began (1:3), and the kingdom has been without a queen for three and a half years. It has taken, therefore, over two years for the king fully to forget about Vashti and to gather candidates to replace her. He is clearly in no rush. Following such a leisurely preparation period, the subsequent haste with which certain actions are performed is unexpected. Hegai rushes to begin Esther's cosmetic regimen (v. 9). Then, after she comes to the king, the narrative pacing itself accelerates. In rapid succession, Ahasuerus is quick to decide that he loves her, to choose her, to crown her, and to throw her a party (vv. 16-18). Moreover, the various elements of the beauty ritual are demarcated with temporal precision: exactly six months for one treatment and six months for another (v. 12). The pacing during the subsequent selection period is as regular as clockwork; "girl by girl" they go, one per night, with morning and evening each bringing its separate activity (vv. 12, 14; author's translation). All of this current action rests against the backdrop of ancient history. The note about Mordecai's ancestry (vv. 5-6) serves to give temporal perspective to all the kingdom's happenings, reminding the reader embroiled in the current drama how quickly world empires (even the present one?) tend to come and go.

The setting undergoes a shift in perspective. As the episode commences, the action moves from the official government chambers of palace administration, shifting to focus upon common folk, particularly upon an individual family. This change, however, is not as great as one might anticipate. As residents of the citadel of Susa, Mordecai and Esther were probably among the guests at King Ahasuerus's and Queen Vashti's drinking parties. As is time, space is likewise carefully delineated throughout the episode. There are two distinct places for the young women, separated by boundaries physical (brick walls) and experiential (being a king's playmate) (v. 14). Mordecai has his space also, but it is relegated to the periphery; as Esther moves to the center of political power, all he remains able to do is to look in from the outside (vv. 11, 19). In the end, Esther is in the "house of royalty" (v. 16; author's translation), the very place that Vashti threw her party (1:9). Esther physically takes over Vashti's space, just as, politically, she takes over Vashti's rank.

Exegetical Analysis

Verses 5-7 serve to acquaint the reader with Mordecai and Esther. Their introductions are significant. Of the two, Mordecai is presented first: "A man, a Jew, was in the citadel of Susa" (author's translation). That Mordecai is in the citadel, and not in the city, of Susa may indicate that he is a court official of some sort. The fact that the narrative later notes that Mordecai is "at the king's gate" (2:19, 21) further suggests that he may hold some type of position in the court administration, as in the ancient Near East the gate area of a city was the locus for legal and commercial transactions. The first characteristic observed about this individual is his maleness, then immediately following, his nationality (his name itself is not given until later). From the very beginning, the narrative emphasizes Mordecai's Jewishness; his ethnicity is the second most significant trait about him, right after his gender. Earlier the narrative hinted that a variety of ethnic groups inhabited the kingdom, though none was explicitly mentioned by name (1:22). Now this episode begins by showing, in more focused detail, one of these cultures. Esther is introduced by two names: first her Jewish name,

Hadassah, and second her Persian name, Esther. It is the latter, however, by which she will be known throughout the remainder of the story; this is the first and only reference to Hadasseh in the entire book—unlike Daniel, for instance, who is known by his Jewish name rather than his Babylonian name (Dan 1:7). This detail gives a foretaste of how Esther's Jewishness will be eclipsed throughout most of the story. There is also a dichotomy between Mordecai having a good Persian name (Horn 1964) yet also being part of a good Jewish lineage. The names of his ancestors, whether distant or immediate (for various options, cf. Bush 1996, 362-63), are reminiscent of the introduction to Saul in 1 Samuel 9:1, a similarity that will later become significant. Thus, from the beginning, both Mordecai and Esther are presented as both Jewish and Persian, living between two cultures.

That these two characters are not of the dominant nationality suggests their marginality within Persian society. Furthermore, the description of their ancestors as exiles, outside their homeland, renders an additional sense of their liminality. Terms for exile are repeated four times in the Hebrew text of verse 6. Jewishness is therefore correlated with dislocation. Esther is the more marginal of the two figures. She is an orphan, having lost both mother and father, traditionally one of the most destitute types of persons in ancient society (cf. Deut 10:18; Jer 5:28; Zech 7:10; Ps 10:14-18). Although the names of Mordecai's forefathers are given back three generations, the reader knows nothing of Esther's lineage. Her father is not named until much later, at verse 15, and her mother not at all. Not geneological lines, but "the lines of her face and figure ... are most important" to the author (Moore 1971, 26). That Mordecai took the orphan under his wing is a suggestion of kindness, for adopting a child is not a frequent action in the Hebrew Bible. The term indicating his action (*'ōmen*, "brought up") occurs only a handful of times: for Naomi's relationship to her grandson (Ruth 4:16), for the nurses of Jonathan's son (1 Sam 4:4) and of Ahab's seventy sons (2 Kgs 10:1, 5), and, metaphorically, for the nurses of a young child (Num 11:12), and of returning peoples (Isa 49:23). But as the objects of this action of bringing up are of various ages, these other instances are not helpful to determine how old Esther might have been—an infant or an adolescent—when Mordecai accepted responsibility for her. In the face of their marginality, therefore, Mordecai and Esther become family for each other. As no mention is made of other (living) relatives of Mordecai, wife or children, in a certain way he appears as alone in the world as does Esther. She has only him, and he only her. When she is taken to the palace, the separation may be equally difficult for the both of them. Mordecai appears to deal with this separation less stalwartly than does she. A victim of "empty nest syndrome," he cannot quite let her go and continues to monitor her to assuage his own curiosity and worry (v. 11; possibly also v. 19).

A distinctive progression is presented in verse 7. Three elements are noted: Mordecai's adoption, Esther's orphan status, and Esther's physical aspect. They are presented in an inverted, or chiastic, structure: Mordecai brought up Esther > Esther has no parents > Esther is beautiful < Esther has no parents < Mordecai brought up Esther. In a typical chiastic structure, the emphasis is placed upon the center element. Here, that element would be Esther's appearance. But it is an odd linking among the three, not a logical progression at all. What connection does Esther's beauty have with the others? Is her comeliness one of the reasons, along with the death of her parents, that Mordecai chose to adopt his cousin, as this ordering would seem to suggest? The reader might note that no other reason is given; for instance, the text does not state, "Because Mordecai felt sorry for Esther in her orphanhood, he adopted her."

The narrative's mention of Esther's beauty is, at the very least, an explanatory note. It explains why she is among those rounded up for the selection; "beautiful young virgins" are the items sought throughout the empire (2:2); and because Esther fits this criteria, she is taken. But for more than this reason, Esther's beauty serves as an indication of her character and a hint of her upcoming role in this story. Numerous other biblical characters are also described as being physically attractive (for instance, Sarah, Rebekah, David, Bathsheba, Tamar, Absalom, Judith). In biblical literature, therefore, beauty is not merely a physical descriptor but also signals the individual's larger significance. Even Esther's Hebrew name, Hadasseh, which means "myrtle," hints at her attractiveness—she is as sweet as the scent of a myrtle blossom. Two phrases are used to describe Esther's appearance; literally, the girl is "beautiful in form" and "good in appearance." They describe both her visible beauty ("good in appearance") and the shape of her figure ("beautiful in form"). Because biblical narrative generally tends to be terse in its descriptions of physical circumstances, it is noteworthy that not one but two descriptive phrases are used here; it emphasizes that Esther is, indeed, very pretty. The joining of these two phrases also links Esther with previous biblical characters who are also described by means of similar dual phrases. Both Rachel and Joseph are likewise reported to be "beautiful in form and beautiful in appearance," with almost similar terminology (Gen 29:17; 39:6). Abigail is also described with one of these phrases, "beautiful of form," the more rare of the two (1 Sam 25:3). (As being "good" in someone's sight is a favorite concept in the book of Esther, this reason may explain why the author chose to replace "beautiful" with "good" in describing her appearance.) In all three of these instances, the characters' physical aspect, particularly the indication "beautiful in form," explains subsequent actions: why Jacob prefers Rachel to Leah, why Potiphar's wife woos Joseph, and why, along with her cleverness and loyalty, David selects Abigail for a wife. Here in the book of Esther, the introduction of Esther by this same terminology is also used to explain subsequent actions—why Hegai and the king favor her.

It is subsequently reported that Esther gains the favor of Hegai, the chief eunuch governing the young women (vv. 8-9). After first being merely a passive object ("Esther also was taken"), she moves to determine her own fate when she more actively "pleased him and won his favor." Esther is, even at this early point, beginning to be able to read the political situation of the palace. She has already realized that if she desires to succeed, this is the man she must win over. As a result of her initiative, she is given special treatment. Hegai's haste may signify that he starts her beauty treatments early, to give her an advantage over the others (Fox 2001, 31-32). One would assume all the young women would be provided the cosmetics and food (cf. v. 12), but the extra personal servants and the special placement are unique to Esther. There is a play on words in the Hebrew here. The seven servants are described as "chosen young women." Esther is also named by the term expression "young woman," and she is also chosen. So her seven servants parallel her own position. And all of them—servants and Esther—are promoted. Esther's good fortune, therefore, is not hers alone, but also spills over to those who serve her. Like Joseph and Daniel, Esther rises quickly to favor in the foreign court (Gen 39:1-6; Dan 1:3-21). How she matures into a successful courtier will be developed as the story progresses.

This event elucidates the importance of Hegai in the palace environment. What Esther wins, in gaining his approval, is his kindness and devotion (*hesed,* which the NRSV here renders as "favor"). This action signifies that Hegai is now committing himself to Esther, to work for her success in the selection contest. Esther has obtained—and very quickly, no less—the chief steward on her side. Hegai anticipates accurately what Ahasuerus will like; just as Hegai's response to Esther is devotion *(hesed),* the king's response to her is that very same devotion (*hesed*; v. 17). Knowing his monarch's preferences is a sure indicator of his expertise as a palace courtier. This incident reveals how Hegai is really the one with power, the one who predicts the new queen. With his stamp of approval, Esther is a shoo-in for the position.

In this short space of time, Esther has undergone a significant transformation of her situation. She is first in a circumstance that is described especially by deficiency, the lack of both of her parents (v. 7). Now her situation is instead marked by wealth, the recipient of a great abundance of gifts (the verb "to give" occurs twice in the Hebrew in verse 9). Her social circumstances are also rapidly transformed. Esther progresses from being completely alone (v. 7), to having one relative (v. 7), to being one amongst a large group (v. 8), to alone again as she is singled out from that group (v. 9), to being surrounded by servants (v. 9). What a great change all of these transformations must be for such a young person.

The letters of Esther's (Persian) name can also be read as the

Hebrew expression "I hide," introducing the book's emphasis upon hiddenness and revelation (cf. Beal 1997). The pun provided by her name sets up the expectation of concealment, and the reader will continue to wonder throughout the story why this character is hiding. Only in verse 10 does one understand what Esther is hiding, "her people or kindred." The mention of "people" recollects 1:22, which alludes to the many peoples in the kingdom. In this instance "her people" refers to the Jews, a community to whom her cousin Mordecai belongs (v. 5). To whom the term "kindred" refers is less clear; it is a rather odd term to use, for Esther has been introduced as *lacking* kindred. Is Mordecai intending that she conceal him? Or more generally, his genealogy (vv. 5-6)? In any event, the precise combination of these two categories of people appears significant to the narrative, as the same combination is repeated at verse 20 and at 8:6.

Mordecai's concern about his foster daughter is clear, though his emotions are not stated in so many words (v. 11). His reason for pacing before the women's quarters is, literally, "to know the well-being of Esther and what was being done to her." These two phrases indicate that Mordecai is doing two things. First, he is observing how satisfactorily she is doing, the substantial well-being that has come her way, that is, her good fortune (v. 9). Second, he is attempting to know what is happening to her in the palace. As fortunes can change quickly in this environment, as with Vashti's banishment and Esther's current rise in status, Mordecai may fear that Esther's circumstances might change just as quickly again—so he had best be diligent in watching. The second phrase, in the passive mode ("what was being done to her"), also shows how Esther is not fully active; she is as much the recipient of actions as their instigator (v. 9).

An overview of the process of the young women's preparation is provided by verses 12-14. That this process is technically termed an "edict" *(dāt)* gives it the same weight as other edicts in the Persian government throughout the story; these treatments appear to be regarded with a considerable seriousness by the administration. The time frame for the preparation, a full year, is yet an-other of the overblown characteristics of this narrative. A distinction is made between the social categories of the young women. After having her moment with the king, each woman moves into a new social class (no longer a young woman but a concubine), a different physical dwelling (the second house of women), and a different supervisor (no longer Hegai but Shaashgaz). The brief experience of the king's company acts as a watershed, changing the lives of these individual girls in striking and irreversible ways.

Attention must be given to the terminology used to describe the cosmetic treatments provided for these young women (v. 12; also v. 3). The terms translated as "cosmetic treatment" and "cosmetics" are both related to the Hebrew verb *māraq*, which means "to rub," in the sense of cleansing or anointing. Though the description is too vague to permit one to know exactly what the procedure entails, clearly at its heart are treatments that involve some type of massage or fumigation with the fragrant spices over incense burners (Albright 1974). Such treatments with oils and ointments for twelve months would make the scents integral to the young woman's skin. The first ointment noted, "myrrh" *(mōr)*, is a fairly rare word in the Hebrew Bible. Except for a single instance (Exod 30:23), all occurrences of the term are used for sexual situations (for example, Song 1:13; 5:1-13; Prov 7:17; Ps 45:8). The second ointment, "perfumes" *(bōśem)*, refers to some sort of spice or balsam. It is a more common word, used in situations of priestly rites, trading, or wealth, but it is also significantly used at places with sexual innuendo (for example, Song 4:10-16; 5:1-13; 6:2; 8:14). The frequent repetition of both of these terms in the Song of Songs, a roughly contemporaneous composition, suggests overtones of the erotic here in the book of Esther. The sensual and sexual details of the preparation continue to develop the characterization of the bodily self-indulgence of Ahasuerus (wine, and now women). Moreover, the expense devoted to these women—using precious and costly perfumes on so many girls for such an extended treatment—rivals the financial extravagance of the king's first two drinking parties.

Though the vocabulary intimates that the evening's encounter is sexual, such is never explicitly stated by the text. Elsewhere, the Hebrew Bible is not reticent in observing sexual encounters (for instance, with Eve and Adam [Gen 4:1], Jacob and Leah and Rachel [Gen 29:21, 23, 30], Hannah and Elkanah [1 Sam 1:19], and Abishag and David [1 Kgs 1:4]). One therefore might expect that if the activities were sexual, that fact would be noted. The statement about King Ahasuerus "delighting" in a young woman (v. 14) is not helpful in elucidating this matter, as the Hebrew verb *ḥāpaṣ* signifies merely a general desire or pleasure. Using the same term, later Ahasuerus will "delight" to honor a person (6:6, 7, 9 [twice], 11). The sequence is the same in both of these instances: he delights in a person, which then moves him to bestow an honor on the person (here, on the young woman; in chapter 6, on Mordecai). Therefore, in this scene, exactly what occurs overnight with the king remains a matter of speculation.

There is a certain irony in King Ahasuerus's calling by name the young women in whom he takes pleasure. The girls' fortunes depend, at least partially, upon the king remembering their names. This procedure represents, from their perspective, a risky situation. Recall that Ahasuerus's mental acuity is not strong; he is always asking for advice and cannot think for himself. Nor does his memory itself prove to be sound, as he apparently forgets Vashti (until he remembers her much later; 2:1), he forgets to honor Mordecai (6:3), and he cannot remember that he authorized a ban against an entire population (7:5). With regard to Esther, though he presumably calls her by her name Esther, he really does not know her actual name, which is Hadassah. In other words, that he does not know her Jewish name signifies that he does not know her Jewishness. The action of summoning Esther "by name" is thus an act both of revelation and of concealment.

The daily life of the typical young woman is based upon passivity and obedience. Along with the cosmetic treatments, which are "given" to her, most likely all of her needs are likewise provided, without requiring active determination on her part. Obedience is expected of these young girls. If Esther serves as an accurate model, the general expectations for them consist of keeping quiet (v. 10), following others' advice (Mordecai's, Hegai's), depending upon others (the eunuchs, her servants, the king), and coming when called. Emphasized for all the young women is the last, responding to being called. Each woman is called first in the general summons (2:2-3, 8), then in her individual summons to the king when it becomes her turn (v. 13), then, if she is lucky and liked by the king, she is summoned a third time (v. 14). It seems that Ahasuerus is still trying to requisition women, even though that proved to be a highly unsuccessful strategy with regard to Vashti. Is he unable to learn from experience? Or, because these young girls are immature and inexperienced, does he expect that they will respond differently to his bidding? Esther does choose to come at the king's summons. Later, though, she inverts his expectation of how young women should behave by first coming when she is *not* called (5:1-2) and then daring instead to summon him (5:4, 8).

What occurs when Esther goes in to King Ahasuerus is described in verses 15-18. Why the narrative repeats the information about Mordecai's adoption of Esther (vv. 7, 15) is not clear. Surely the reader would remember who he is and what he has done from just a few verses earlier. Perhaps the purpose is to emphasize a shift in paternity: Mordecai took Abihail's place, acting as Esther's foster father, and now Hegai is taking Mordecai's place, acting as a father figure in Mordecai's absence. Esther's young life has consisted of a series of being taken from one place to another, the completion of which occurs here. The Hebrew verb *lāqaḥ*, "to take," links them all. First she is taken by Mordecai upon her parents' death (v. 7; the NRSV translates as "adopted" in this circumstance), then she is taken to the palace (v. 8), then another report on Mordecai's taking of her (v. 15), and finally she is taken to the king (v. 16). Esther has been chauffeured from one place to another and transferred to the control of one man after another (Abihail, Mordecai, Hegai, Ahasuerus).

Though no explicit speech by Esther is noted throughout this entire episode, her quietness is emphasized at verse 15. Along with twice reporting that Esther does not speak of her origins (vv. 10, 20), now the text hints more strongly at her silence. It is Hegai whom the reader hears. Like Vashti, speech is not provided to Esther in this initial introduction to the character (though she later becomes quite vocal); the reader is told only of her physical actions. That Esther wins the favor of "all who saw her" further renders the impression that she, at this point, may be seen more than heard. That she gains this approval by those who are merely *seeing* her (versus knowing her or hearing her or speaking with her or the like) suggests that the primary basis for that opinion is still her physical attractiveness.

It is not clear how the remark that Esther brings nothing except what Hegai suggests for her night with the king should be understood (v. 15). Is her asking for nothing a sign of lack of imagination (she cannot fathom what might help her), or a sign of wisdom (she knows to follow the advice of a wise courtier), or a sign of confidence (she knows that she, by her own self, has what it takes to succeed and that she needs no extra props)? So when the strategy works, does one credit Esther or Hegai? Perhaps they choose to strategize together to bring about the result, just as Esther and Mordecai later do when hatching ideas about Purim (9:29-32). In any event, the fact that Esther brings less than the other young women have brought probably makes her uniqueness stand out to Ahasuerus.

Verse 17 exhibits a nice parallelism, significant because parallelism is seen more often in Hebrew verse than in prose: "And the king loved Esther [A] more than all the women [B], and she lifted up favor and devotion before him [A´] more than all the virgins [B´]" (author's translation). The Hebrew term for "love," *'āhab,* can signify a variety of types of love, from casual affection to overwhelming devotion, including sexual love but not necessarily so. The term is used with significance in this context, for it suggests that Ahasuerus holds affection for Esther not expressed in his feelings for Vashti. Loving is also a greater response and of a different type than the "delighting" expected from the king (v. 14). Though the narrative gives the sense that Ahasuerus may have intended to try out some women more than one night, with Esther he instantly understands that he has found the right individual. His response also differs from the "admiring" rendered by the bystanders on account of Esther's beauty (v. 15). One might understand his reaction in one of two ways. One possibility is that, as this king has shown himself to be superficial and foolish, his response to a pretty face is immediately to profess love and devotion, without getting to know the woman. Those who see her beauty and respond merely with admiration offer the more sensible response. A second possibility is that Ahasuerus, during his night with Esther, has gotten to know her character, beyond the physical appearance. Perhaps his increased affection is a response to his knowing her more fully, that her integrity is fine enough to warrant such a committed response.

Along with the king's love, Esther also wins his "favor" *(ḥen)* and his "devotion" *(ḥesed)*. This phrase combines the judgments of two other constituencies with Ahasuerus's judgment. Esther has already gained Hegai's "devotion" *(ḥesed;* v. 9) and the onlookers' "favor" *(ḥen;* v. 15). (Later the narrative will use the same terminology to describe how she wins Ahasuerus's favor again [5:2].) By this time it is becoming clear how adept this young woman is at garnering approval. That Esther is reported to have the king's loyalty and devotion, along with his love, gives the impression that this occurrence is more than a one-night stand, that he intends it as commitment. The suggestion of such loyalty contrasts with the lack of commitment Ahasuerus showed toward Vashti.

Throughout these verses the repetition of "royalty" *(malkût)* is noteworthy. The term is used twice in verse 16: Esther is taken "to the house of his royalty ... in the seventh year of his royalty" (author's translation). Though she has been living in the palace compound for many months, the effect of this repetition is to highlight that young Esther is now entering the most powerful, the most "royal" place; she is now playing in the big leagues. Moreover, this royal aspect is specifically indicated as the king's possession. But when the "crown of royalty" *(keter-malkût)* is placed upon Esther's head, this royal authority is transferred onto her as well and she will henceforth also be royal (v. 17). At the designation "crown of royalty," the reader cannot help but recall the previous instance of this same term, the item that Vashti refused to wear when modeling for the party-goers (1:11), and draw a comparison with Esther. The fact that Esther willingly accepts the role that Vashti rejected highlights the difference in personality between these two women. This correlation is made explicitly in the second part of the verse: Esther is crowned "instead of Vashti." The comparison expresses, perhaps, a hope on Ahasuerus's part that Esther will turn out to be a different type of queen than was her predecessor. Vashti, though supposedly off the scene these four years, still continues to linger (2:4, 17). She will keep on being remembered, through Esther's presence, in that all that Esther will do henceforth is "instead of Vashti."

The wedding banquet is the fourth drinking party in the book (v. 18). This party is for the same groups of people as was the first, "for all his officials and his servants" (author's translation; cf. 1:3). How the designation of it being "great" in light of the previous three is not clear; certainly the six-month affair that was the first party would be hard to top! It would be difficult, also, to improve upon the lavishness of the second. Even fewer details are given about this wedding party than for Vashti's party, as the narrative notes the guest list but not even its location. This drinking party functions to set things right again after the Vashti debacle. Now with a new compliant young queen on the throne, it represents a sigh of relief by the Persian administration that patriarchy is once again secure in the land—sealed with a toast (Beal 1999, 37).

Details of this drinking party prefigure the celebration of Purim occurring later in the story. Just as this one is named, it will be another "Esther's banquet." At the present drinking party, Ahasuerus calls for a giving of rest, or "a holiday." This term, *hănāhâ*, is a noun related to the verb *nûah*, which appears also at 9:16, 17, and 18 to refer to the Jews' rest from their enemies during their celebration. The gift giving at this party therefore anticipates the Jews' giving of gifts during Purim (9:19, 22). The action of celebration, combined with rest and generosity to others, links these two events, even though the reason for and the participants in the celebrations differ. Recall that Esther already has the general population's approbation (v. 15). Because of her they now receive a holiday, gifts, and amnesty, which—like a politician's tax cuts—probably adds to their affection and approval toward her. Within the Jewish population in particular, such popular endorsement would incline them to regard favorably her requests of them (4:16; 8:5-8; 9:12-14, 29-32).

At verses 19-20 the focus splits between Mordecai and Esther. Though what is meant by the reference to the young women being gathered "a second time" is not completely clear, it most probably pertains to the gathering into the second harem (v. 14) and indicates that these two events are simultaneously occurring in different venues; that is, while the girls are moving from one harem to the next in the palace, outside the palace compound Mordecai is at the king's gate. Even if this designation of the royal gate is more figurative than literal (i.e., designating an occupational rather than a physical position [cf. Berlin 2001a, 31-32; Bush 1996, 372-73]), it still functions to draw a distinction between the situations of Esther and her foster father. One would expect that Esther's progression of changes in households (from Abihail's, to Mordecai's, to Hegai's, to Ahasuerus's) be complete now. But with this reference back to Mordecai's connection with her, it appears that Esther is still living between two family systems, that of Ahasuerus and that of Mordecai, rather than being securely in the former. Both of these men continue to have influence over her. Just as Mordecai has been thinking about Esther from afar (v. 11), so it is now suggested that she is also continuing to remember him. Esther stands as an example of the impossibility of completely leaving a previous family system when moving to enter into a new family situation.

This is the second time that the narrative reports that Esther follows Mordecai's advice not to divulge "her kindred or her people," repeating the information from verse 10. The reiteration lends particular weight to this detail. Though in the bustle of palace life it would probably be possible to keep her origins unknown (Fox 2001, 33), the reason why Mordecai so emphatically wishes Esther's silence is not at all clear. The Persian kingdom has proven itself to be open to other cultures (1:22), and Mordecai himself does not follow such advice, for he informs his colleagues that he is Jewish (3:4). When Esther finally does reveal her ethnic background and her familial connections, they are of no consequence (7:3-10; 8:1-2); her secreted information is not viewed negatively, nor does it cause her to be banished from the throne. One might conclude that Mordecai is not fully knowledgeable of how to behave in this kingdom and especially in its palace environs, a characteristic that will become more evident in the following two episodes. When counseling Esther thusly, Mordecai appears to be speaking more out of his own worries about intolerance than providing her with beneficial or necessary advice.

The latter portion of verse 20 reads, literally, "And the word of Mordecai Esther did, accordingly she was in fidelity with him." The second citation of a "word" (*ma'ămar*) recalls the instance when this rare term was used previously to refer to King Ahasuerus's "word" regarding Queen Vashti (1:15). Both of these "words," these behests, are made by men to women (Vashti, Esther) who are supposed to be under their authority. The term *'āmĕnâ* ("brought up" in the NRSV) commonly means "truly, faithfully," and this meaning may be more appropriate for this context. The statement is emphasizing how Esther is acting loyally in following Mordecai's desires. She is being faithful to him. This remark, therefore, displays Esther's good character; it is a mark of her personal integrity toward her cousin, or even possibly her gratitude for what he had done for her. At the close of this scene, the repetition of Esther's obedience and subservience to Mordecai provides an emphasized contrast with the next time she will appear, when she will have matured and will be more demanding, forceful, self-determined, and less deferential to her foster father.

Theological and Ethical Analysis

This episode reflects the interplay between the powerful and the powerless. Ahasuerus is one of the powerful, holding control over the inhabitants of his kingdom. How great must a man think he is, to presume that he can demand such wholesale attention from others? One cannot help but think of modern heads of state who have exhibited such complete control over their citizenry (Crawford 1999, 887). Yet such power possesses the danger of making one vain, in thinking that others will want one's company. Any attention and affection bestowed upon such individuals tends not to be given freely but conscripted, bought by command and expensive gifting. In contrast, Esther and Mordecai represent the comparatively powerless, those who do not have control over their own destinies, who must go and come when the authorities say so. And in broader terms, Esther's predicament reflects that of the Jews as a whole. As Levenson contends, "as they have lost their king and their land and taken up residence in a foreign country, so has she lost her father and her mother, become adopted by her cousin, and taken a foreign name" (1997, 56). A dichotomy in the power structure is evidenced on the national level as well as the personal level—the mighty Persian Empire against the weak Jewish nation.

The episode represents not only the power of position, but also the power of family. At the level of the individual family, Mordecai demonstrates how one can manage an unconventional household and love a child who is not one's own. His concern for Esther represents every parent's worry about her or his children. As children get older, they drift further out of one's control; all a parent can do can only be done from afar, watching, pacing, and hoping that things turn out well for them. The story reflects the persevering nature of family relationships. Even when family members are physically distant from one another, the familial bond holds tight.

The selection process paints a picture of a society that puts great value upon physical beauty. Yet surely there is injustice in judging persons on the basis of something over which they have little actual control, twelve months of marinating in perfume notwithstanding. The activities of this episode highlight the inequities that beauty brings. It exhibits an unfairness that is often part of universal human experience, that the attractive have always gotten to move ahead two free spaces in the game of life. Yet the beauty of these young women may prove in the long run to be a disadvantage in preventing them from living as full lives as they otherwise might have. Contemporary Western culture continues this quest for beauty and youth. Though so many search for physical beauty (six months of plastic surgery and six months of liposuction), the story raises the question of whether the beautiful are really any better off in the end. After all, only one lucky individual wins the handsome prince and gets to be queen.

What the king requires of his people is nothing less than their exploitation. The enlistment of the young women is not voluntary but conscripted, and Ahasuerus will possess the losing contestants as well as the winner. The effects upon the society as a whole must likewise be considered. With the loss of their young women, countless families will be missing their daughters and countless young men will be missing potential wives. All of this hardship for the many is to salve one man's vanity and egotism, to pay for a personal mistake he made in his first marriage. Moreover, this action entails great waste. Just as his extravagant parties wasted financial resources (1:1-8), the king's process wastes human resources. All of these women could have been productive lmembers of society, bringing their mental and physical strength to the needs of the people. And in a moral sense, it is hard to commend a society that chooses to sacrifice its children for the capricious needs of the state. A good indicator of any culture is how well it cares for its young and its helpless. Judged according to such a standard, this kingdom would fail miserably.

Though admittedly a matter of conjecture, it is impossible to help but wonder what the lives of these many young women would be like. One might contend, as is common in interpretation of the book, that in living amongst the wealth of this kingdom all of the women's physical needs would be met, that life would probably be more comfortable than outside the citadel. Whereas the first year of preparations might be fun for a teenage girl interested in makeup and clothes, curious about her emergent sexuality, residing in the harem for the second and subsequent years may be less enjoyable. Though the cage is gilded, it still remains a cage. Yet perhaps the situation would not be completely dissatisfactory. One cannot discount the human capacity to adapt and thrive. The all-female community in the harem might well prove to be a place of female empowerment. For instance, women's colleges and religious convents were formed because of systems no less patriarchal than the Persian kingdom, women being prohibited from matriculating at men's universities or from serving in the ordained priesthood. But many women in such female institutions come to find them to be positive, even desirable, environments in and of themselves, places where women can experience their fuller potential without the need to succumb to male expectations. It is certainly possible for the caged bird to sing.

The characters reflect the difficulties and choices facing persons who live between two worlds. In one case it is the world of gender. Hegai, Shaashgaz, and all the other eunuchs (1:10) live between female and male worlds. They are not fully men, and though they live within the realm of the palace women, they are not women either. Theirs is the situation of all persons who do not fit neatly into heterosexual categories. Mordecai also, lacking the expected wife and children of the typical ancient Near Eastern male, represents an ambiguous sexual identity. In another case, it is the world of culture. Both Esther and Mordecai represent multiethnic individuals, those living between two (or more) cultures. In the face of this challenge, Esther lives out of only one of those identities and "hides" the other. In the context of our current multiethnic, transgendered societies, the story of Esther raises various questions. Is one always forced to choose one identity over another and live completely in it? To what extent do people lose their first identity, lose their "name," when accommodating to a second identity? Can community be maintained between those who choose to accommodate and those who do not? To what extent does discrimination, either actual or anticipated, act to keep one silent? The last concern is especially pertinent at this current, post-Shoah, point in history. Though the book of Esther was written before the development of anti-Judaism in the ancient world, Mordecai's advice of silence rings true today after the world has experienced centuries of the atrocities of anti-semitism. History has shown that assimilation does not always safeguard one from harm in times of genocide; keeping silent does not necessarily protect.

MORDECAI VERSUS HAMAN (2:21–3:15)

The episode commences as Mordecai, with the assistance of Esther, reveals a plot against the king's life about which he has learned. Ahasuerus gives the courtier Haman a grand promotion, but Mordecai's refusal to honor Haman properly precipitates his revenge; he convinces the king to issue a decree for the Persian population to attack and destroy Mordecai's people. The conflict that will take the remainder of the story to resolve is here initiated.

Literary Analysis

The focus in this episode lies upon Mordecai and Haman, with Esther and Ahasuerus appearing on stage but playing only minor roles. This situation reverses that of the previous episode, in which Esther functioned as the primary character, with Mordecai appearing only briefly. The cousins' working together as they divulge the assassination plot prefigures their cooperative efforts later (chapter 9). The observation that Mordecai is at the king's gate is a resumptive phrase; 2:19 reports that he was sitting at the gate during Esther's events, and now 2:21 repeats that he is stationing himself there once again (or is still there). At 3:1, Haman, the last of the story's protagonists to appear, is presented in a fashion reminiscent of Mordecai's prior introduction (2:5-6). After Haman's encounter with Mordecai, attention shifts predominantly to him alone in his drafting of the new edict. This episode continues a progression with regard to characterization. The initial episode focused upon the political importance of Ahasuerus (1:1-8), then Esther's importance was the focus of the episode immediately previous to this one (2:5-20), and now focus is upon the importance of Haman. Not until considerably later in the story will Mordecai's importance be stressed (6:10-11).

The setting of the action likewise shifts as one enters this episode. In the last episode all action took place, save for the mention of Mordecai's response (2:11, 19), completely within the palace walls. Now, however, the setting begins outside the palace. The event with the eunuchs is at an in-between space, the threshold—neither in nor out. As the keepers of this space, they function as marginalized characters. Even Mordecai at this point is interpersonally marginal, shut out from his foster daughter's new life on the inside. The setting begins to slip from the margins to the center with Mordecai's report (Beal 1999, 41) but does not do so fully until Haman's conversation with Ahasuerus, presumably in the palace. The broader kingdom comes into focus as the edict is dispatched to the provinces. The episode concludes with the two levels of space presented simultaneously in the final sentence (3:15b). The camera records a visually artistic split frame, one side representing the image of what is occurring in the king's chambers and the other side representing the image of what is occurring in the city streets.

The time when Mordecai learns of the plot is not clear. Certainly it occurs some time after the coronation, as Esther is now referred to as the queen (2:22), but how long afterward is not stated. Furthermore, the narrative gives no indication of how much time elapses between the archival documentation (2:23) and the altercation (beginning at 3:2). The sole certain indication of date in the episode is at 3:7, when Haman casts his lots during "the twelfth year of King Ahasuerus." Almost five years have passed since Esther's coronation. Because Haman will prove to be an impatient individual (5:9–6:14), he probably would be unable to wait very long to punish Mordecai. Therefore, the events of Mordecai's refusal to bow most likely occur directly before the casting of lots and the preparation of the new edict.

Exegetical Analysis

Two encounters occur at the "king's gate" in this episode (2:21; 3:2). The location of the gate, either of the city or of the royal estate, carries importance in the biblical tradition. It is a public meeting place where elders, judges, important citizens, guards, and even kings are said to frequent, a place where justice is carried out and divine presence might be expected (e.g., Gen 19:1; Deut 21:19; 1 Kgs 22:10; Prov 31:23, 31). Why Mordecai is there is not clear. Not until 3:3 is there the hint that perhaps he is one of the king's attendants, for he is chastised by the king's servants for not acting properly. But even then his occupation is not clear, for Mordecai is never literally described as one of Ahasuerus's servants or officials. When the king's servants speak to him, it is difficult to determine whether they are addressing one of their colleagues in the king's employ or merely a common citizen who is causing a ruckus in a public place, though the former seems more likely (3:3-4).

As eunuchs, the conspirators Bigthan and Teresh occupy a liminal sexual space, the threshold between male and female (2:21). Here they also occupy a liminal physical space: the threshold between the royal palace and the outer city. The presentation of Bigthan and Teresh fits with that of other servants throughout the book. The servants in this kingdom appear to be well respected and valued, if one can understand their being included on party lists as an indication of generous treatment (1:3). Furthermore, that this narrative almost always provides servants' names, which is not typical for biblical literature, gives an impression of their importance as individuals. Yet the fact that servants often act as a unit (1:10, 21; 4:4, 12; 7:10) or exhibit unexplained actions, as here, makes them appear as more than mere plot devices. The reader is not told why Bigthan and Teresh, the two individuals who guard the threshold, become angry with King Ahasuerus. Anger is a theme in the book of Esther, but clear reasons are provided in the cases of the other characters who become incensed. Even less clear is why Bigthan and Teresh become so enraged as to desire the king's demise.

The reader cannot be sure how Mordecai becomes aware of the eunuchs' conspiracy, for 2:21-23 reads more as a stylized account, including only enough information to give the reason why Mordecai is honored later (6:1-11). Though it is tempting to assume that Mordecai overhears them plotting, the text merely reports that "the matter came to the knowledge of Mordecai" (2:22). Is he lucky enough to be in the right place at the right time, or does someone involved in the intrigue leak the information to him? Is he an official, therefore, one whose obligation it is to take responsibility for such threats to the safety of the kingdom? But if so, one would expect that he could report such activity directly to the court and not have to be dependent upon Esther as a conduit. Moreover, in Mordecai's reporting the information to her, there is no mention of the servants who elsewhere function as intermediaries between Esther and Mordecai (4:5-9). Some interpreters question why Esther's relaying the tip "in the name of Mordecai" would not reveal her Jewish identity to the king and the court, considering this detail to be a possible "slip in narrative logic"

(Fox 2001, 40) or a comedic touch (Levenson 1997, 64). Another option is that in the five years between this incident and Haman's edict, this detail simply slips the mind of the forgetful Ahasuerus.

In Haman's introduction, the emphasis upon hierarchy in this story—who is above whom—is evident in the remark about Haman's new status as superceding his colleagues. The narrative observes how Ahasuerus promotes him to a "seat above all the officials who were with him." Up to this point one would have supposed that Memucan is the leader of the highest palace officials, in light of his singular leadership on the Vashti affair (1:14-22). Yet now this individual Haman appears out of the woodwork. The reader cannot be sure whether Memucan has been demoted or a new position has been created for Haman; or whether Haman has been in the court throughout these past events, observing all that has occurred and getting to know the new queen; or whether he is now coming new to the court from elsewhere.

As for Mordecai and Esther (2:5-6, 15), both Haman's parentage and his ethnic identity are provided: "Haman, son of Hammedatha the Agagite" (3:1). This notation is significant for two reasons. First, one must note that Haman is not Persian but Agagite; he is no more of the ethnic dominant group than are the Jewish Esther and Mordecai. That foreigners are appointed to such a high rank hints at a kingdom administration that is not only open to, but also trusting of, those who are of different ethnic heritages. Esther, of course, has been elevated to the status of queen, but without the palace knowing of her ethnic difference. As it is stated so matter-of-factly, one may presume, in contrast, that all know of Haman's heritage. Both of them are foreigners who have done quite well for themselves. Second, that Haman is Agagite throws the situation into the realm of old rivalries and ethnic animosities. Agag was the king of the Amelekite people during the reign of Saul, and Amelekites are portrayed as enemies of the Israelites in various biblical traditions (Exod 17:8-16; Deut 25:19; Num 24:7). First Samuel 15:1-33, which reports the military encounter between Saul and Agag, particularly resonates with the Esther story. The priest Samuel informs Saul that YHWH wants him to punish the Amalekites. Rather than following the divine command to destroy everything, however, Saul spares King Agag and all the best animals for a sacrifice to YHWH. For his transgression the crown is taken from Saul and Samuel kills Agag. Not only is Mordecai, like Saul, a member of the tribe of Benjamin, but the earlier story hinges upon disobedience and great slaughter, also significant elements in the book of Esther. (For fuller discussions of the connections, see Bush 1996, 384-85; McKane 1961.)

Haman expects all to bow to him. Mordecai, however, refuses (3:2). Oddly, the narrative does not provide a reason for his refusal. This is one of the most significant points of the plot of the story, as Mordecai single-handedly is responsible for causing, ultimately, the edict declaring the Jews' destruction. The reader might expect to be told such a key point of information—why Mordecai insists upon being so stubborn—but is left guessing. Various options are possible. It is frequently suggested that Mordecai will not bow to a foreign ruler because he is Jewish. Yet there are no rules against doing so in Israelite legal tradition, and other Israelites have no qualms about bowing to human rulers (e.g., Gen 23:7; 43:26-28; 2 Sam 14:4; 1 Kgs 1:16), nor does Esther hesitate to prostrate herself to the king. Another possibility is that Mordecai resists giving homage to an ancient enemy, one whose ancestors were at odds with his own ancestors. Support for this option may be found at 3:10, where Haman is again referred to as an Agagite, the one at enmity with the Jews. There is no need to define his lineage again at this point, unless it were to suggest that ancient rivalries lie, at least to some degree, behind the present dispute. Since this scene immediately follows Mordecai's revelation of the assassination plot, another possible reason is that he thinks that he himself should have received Haman's new post. Or perhaps he is simply arrogant and too proud to bow down to another individual. For whatever reason, Mordecai's determination not to comply is persistent; despite attempts to persuade him otherwise, he remains steadfast in his decision (3:4).

The fact that it is actually Ahasuerus's wish, and not merely that of Haman, that subjects are to bow makes Mordecai a study in contrasts. He shows an especially high loyalty to the king in the incident with the eunuchs, which immediately precedes this one, going to considerable trouble to make sure that the occurrence is properly reported. Yet here he exhibits disloyalty to that same king with his disobedience to the much less demanding command to bow. Just as no reason is provided as to why Mordecai will not obey, no reason is given as to why Ahasuerus has issued such a mandate. The narrative does not tell whether, for instance, it was customary to bow to Haman's predecessor, or whether this is a new practice following Haman's promotion. The terminology used to refer to Ahasuerus's request is unexpected. Designations used elsewhere in the book to indicate the king's commands are *dāt* ("edict"), *dābār* ("word"), and *ma'ămar* ("saying"). Here, and only here, his command is referred to as *miṣwâ,* a commandment or an obligation. This is a term that developed in Israelite literature to designate divine commandments, YHWH's demands upon the people, as well as merely human commissions. In a few other instances, a king gives this type of commandment; note, for instance, Hezekiah's command for the people's silence (2 Kgs 18:36), or David's (and YHWH's) command for the Levites' actions in worship (2 Chr 29:25). The parallels suggest that this command is a personal decision of Ahasuerus, in contrast to the official Persian edicts that are described elsewhere throughout the story.

The role of "the king's servants who were at the king's gate" is more noteworthy than it appears at first glance. They are the obedient ones who perform immediately and without question that which their monarch commands (3:2). And they are the ones who try to convince Mordecai to follow suit (3:3). Why they feel it necessary to inform Haman of Mordecai's noncompliance is unclear, but this information does reveal that Haman has remained previously unaware of Mordecai's upright stature—he needs to be *told* of it. It is only after their notification that Haman finally sees Mordecai (3:5). The text literally states "to see whether Mordecai's words would stand," an allusive phrase: neither Mordecai nor his word will bend (3:4). That Mordecai informs the servants of his Jewish identity may be an attempt to garner their sympathy. Perhaps they are taking it upon themselves to try to defend Mordecai to Haman, to explain his words (that is, his situation) to Haman. But the servants also inform Haman that Mordecai is Jewish (the Hebrew text at 3:6 is in the active voice, "for they reported to him Mordecai's people"). Are the servants, presumably being neither Jewish nor Amalekite, well enough informed to be aware that Benjaminites have hated Agagites for centuries? If so, they may be using the ancient rivalry to ingratiate themselves with the new powerbroker in the royal administration. More likely, however, they are not even cognizant of such non-Persian intertribal rivalries. In any case, if the servants had not snitched, Haman would have remained none the wiser about Mordecai. Therefore, they also, along with Mordecai, bear some responsibility for Haman's subsequent response.

Haman, of course, is infuriated; he is literally "filled with anger" (3:5). As the reader will see throughout the story, Haman's inner emotions and thoughts are revealed more than those of any other character, and this is the first instance of this characterization. Yet just as Mordecai's reasons for noncompliance are not explained, exactly why Haman is so angry is not fully clear. What aspect of his character does Mordecai offend? Instead of being concerned about disloyalty to the crown, which Mordecai's refusal actually is (it is Ahasuerus's, and not Haman's, command that Mordecai disobeys), Haman reads Mordecai's actions as a direct affront against *him* (3:5). He is not concerned with Ahasuerus's reputation, but with his own honor. Nor does he want to bloody his own hands; he would rather have the people of Persia do his dirty work while he parties (3:15). Haman has quickly developed pride and egotism in his new position; attempting to emulate Ahasuerus, he yearns to appear king-like. Recall that the king's reason for throwing his drinking parties was for his own aggrandizement, an extension of his pride and egotism (1:4, 8). Just as the king does things in a grand way, inviting many guests and serving them for a extended period, Haman is not satisfied with punishing a single individual but insists upon reacting in grand style (3:6). Absolutely everyone will notice. But one thing that Haman has not learned from the king is generosity.

Ahasuerus is able to find a way to stoke his ego and give benefit to the many at the same time. Haman, however, can only pamper his own ego by bringing destruction upon the many.

In Haman's response, the personal becomes corporate. This incident begins as one person's dislike of another—or perhaps merely that one person's excessive liking of himself. The Jews as a whole are affected only as they are connected to Mordecai, "the people of Mordecai" (3:6, twice). The Jews, one might note, are not a religious category; they are not linked by devotion to the same deity and faith traditions, but instead they are linked by genealogy, i.e., those people who are related to Mordecai. Jews in the book of Esther are treated as an ethnic, not a religious, group. Moreover, there is an emphasis upon the absolute totality of their destruction. Haman's target is, in a single chilling phrase, "all the Jews who are in all the kingdom of Ahasuerus" (3:6, author's translation).

Parallels can be drawn among the various characters. In many ways, Mordecai functions as a corresponding character to Vashti. Both engage in disobedience to a demand of King Ahasuerus, Vashti to appear and Mordecai to bow. A group of servants attempts to persuade each to follow the king's command, but to no avail. Neither tells her or his reasons for so doing, and ultimately the reader is left to guess what the reasons might be. Even though Mordecai appears more frequently than Vashti, by the end of the story his personality remains almost as inscrutable as that of Vashti in her single appearance. Ultimately, with regard to both, the act of an individual has severe ramifications upon an entire group, Vashti on the kingdom's women, and Mordecai on the kingdom's Jews. Though both Mordecai and Vashti do not anticipate the consequences of their choices, nonetheless their single decisions cause suffering to many. Haman parallels characteristics of Bigthan and Teresh. His desire to "lay a hand on" *(lišloḥ yād)* Mordecai is the precise phrase used earlier to describe the intent of the traitors as they plot to "lay a hand on" *(lišloḥ yād)* the king (2:21; 3:6; cf. also 6:2, where this same phrase is repeated; author's translations). Furthermore, Bigthan and Teresh's punishment of being hanged on the gallows prefigures Haman's final end

(7:10). As Haman is now described as intending the very same action as that of the criminals, the expectation is, very subtly, being established that Haman is also a criminal. His intended deed, like their intended deed, is ultimately an act of treason against the throne. Neither party, fortunately, is ultimately successful.

It is reported how Haman has a lot cast to determine a date for the destruction of the Jews (3:7-11), perhaps using bowls and instruments similar to modern-day dice (Hallo 1983). Though one might expect that he would make certain to have any necessary royal approval before casting the lot, Haman is apparently fully confident enough to wait until after doing so to convince Ahasuerus of the necessity to eradicate this segment of the population. That silver changes hands is a significant incentive—Haman pays for the death he desires (3:9).

Haman's rhetoric is masterful; he speaks quite persuasively (3:8-9). His goal is to make the personal corporate. Haman takes a grievance against a single individual and uses it to draw generalities about, and ultimately to punish, an entire population. Recall the text's earlier view of respected cultural groups living throughout the Persian Empire and of an official administration accommodating their uniqueness (1:22), and how Jews blend so well into Persian society that coworkers cannot distinguish them without being so informed (3:4). Haman, however, works to present a very different portrait of ethnic otherness throughout the realm.

In his speech, Haman twice begins with facts that are more or less true, then twists those facts into blatant falsehoods (3:8). He begins, "There is a certain people," which is true: the Jews are an ethnic group just like the many other "certain peoples" living "among the peoples in all the provinces of [the] kingdom." But referring to the Jews as "scattered and separated" puts a negative spin on this fact, presenting them (inaccurately) as unassimilated. Haman continues, "Their laws are different from those of every other people." This statement is accurate, if one considers the Torah as a legal code shared by no other ethnic group. But continuing that "they do not keep the king's laws" is a lie. Mordecai and Esther, if they can be considered representative Jews, fully obey the king's commands (for handsome virgins to come to the citadel for the queen selection) and even save his life. Moreover, note how Haman dehumanizes the Jews. Stating that their laws differ, literally "from [those of] all people," subtly insinuates that the Jews themselves are not people, not fully human. And Haman never names *who* this people is, just "a certain people." He depersonalizes them by presenting them to Ahasuerus as faceless and nameless, for it is much easier to destroy a faceless, anonymous group. Throughout his address, Haman is clearly and consciously working to create prejudice.

The conclusion that Haman draws is that it is not "suitable" or appropriate *(šāwāh)* for the king to permit the Jews to live. To understand exactly what he suggests by this statement, it is instructive to consider the other two instances of this rare word in the book. At 5:13, Haman decries that, after he has been honored by the queen, it is not appropriate for Mordecai to defy him. Esther herself later picks up on this language, that the Jews' death is not appropriate to Ahasuerus (7:4). Both of these instances include the concept of proper treatment, proper honor. Therefore, at 3:8, Haman is couching his threat in terms of King Ahasuerus's *honor* (i.e., this certain people not obeying his laws amounts to dishonoring him). However, Haman's later statement about his problem with Mordecai (5:13) reveals that it is really his *own* honor about which he is concerned. One might observe that he nowhere substantiates to the king any physical harm or danger that these people supposedly bring about to the kingdom. It is only damage to pride.

Haman's suggested "solution" is annihilation of this group of people (3:9). His statement is forcefully blunt: "Let it be written to annihilate them" (author's translation). Haman is also careful to use the passive voice. Not spelling out explicitly that it is Haman who is behind it all serves to give this lazy king the idea that he need not do a thing: the king himself should certainly not be made to feel responsible for the deaths of so many! Indeed, throughout his entire speech, Haman demonstrates a discernible savvy in his presentation. Knowing how all things in the palace revolve around Ahasuerus's pleasure, Haman couches his suggestion in terms of what "pleases the king." Knowing that Ahasuerus is self-centered, he begins both phrases in 3:8*b* (not as obvious in the NRSV) and 3:9 by referring to him first: "for the king" and "if to the king it is good" (author's translations). Haman plays right into Ahasuerus's broad ego. Knowing how important laws are to this palace administration and how disobedience is deemed the ultimate crime, Haman presents a set of laws and noncompliance with the king's edicts as the reasons warranting the Jews' destruction.

The amount of Haman's bribe is fantastic. Ten thousand talents could constitute as much as two-thirds the annual income of the entire Persian Empire (Paton 1908, 205-6). Even if Haman is a person of some means, he surely cannot be this wealthy. This sum is one of the overblown details of the story. On the surface there appears to be a discrepancy in detail between 3:9 and 3:11. The former observes that Haman volunteers to pay the ten thousand talents into the royal treasury, but the latter informs us that Ahasuerus replies to Haman, "The money is given to you," suggesting instead that it is the *king* who pays *Haman*. Later, both Mordecai and Esther are under the impression of what is stated in 3:9, that it is indeed Haman who pays up (4:7; 7:4). However, a closer look at 3:11 reveals that it is really not at odds with 3:9, 4:7, and 7:4. The common word *nātan* is the verb used to indicate the action performed on the money, "is given to you" in the NRSV. Though the most common meaning of *nātan* in the passive voice is "to be given," it can also mean "to be set up, to be established." This statement thus can be read as Ahasuerus telling Haman that the money is "established," that is, Ahasuerus expressing agreement with Haman's offer to pay and accepting his bribe. In other words, the king is saying that Haman set everything up just fine—the amount of the bribe is satisfactory, the actions toward the people are acceptable.

That a ruler would agree to the destruction of an entire people, without asking a single question, is another of the unrealistic details of the story. This king, as the reader has seen, is exceptionally accustomed to getting his advice from others under his command (Memucan, 1:13, 21; servants, 2:2-4). At the beginning of the story, Ahasuerus was a relatively young monarch, only in his third year (1:3). Though it is now nine years later, he has regrettably become no wiser in the interim. As previously, he still trusts the information given to him without asking for facts or thinking to make clarifications, permitting his advisors to determine the appropriate royal action and revealing yet again how pliable he is. Haman's "murky reasoning need not truly convince the king. It need only allow the king to feel that he has heard arguments that justify taking the bribe" (Fox 2001, 53). He literally "rubber-stamps" the deal by giving his signet to Haman so that Haman might authorize what he wants in the king's name and with the king's seal (3:10). Ahasuerus seems more foolishly trusting than malevolent, though the price the people of the Persian Empire pay for having such a senseless king is catastrophic.

The actual composition and dispatch of the new edict is recounted in 3:12-15. The process is similar to that used to send out the letters enforcing household patriarchy (1:22). It is translated into all languages and forwarded throughout the kingdom to all jurisdictions. This missive, though, is sent specifically to the regional rulers, "the king's satraps and ... the governors over all the provinces and ... the officials of all the peoples" (3:12), and the order specifies that it is to be read orally (3:14). Although the edict is recorded "in the name of King Ahasuerus," the reader knows that it is really by Haman's authorship and that it is he who stamps it with "the king's ring," for it is composed "according to all that Haman commanded" (3:12).

The slaughter this edict orders is complete (3:13). That three forceful verbs ("to destroy, to kill, and to annihilate") are used indicates the thoroughness of the violence; that all demographic categories are included ("all Jews, young and old, women and children") makes it clear that the entire population is to be wiped out. The timing of the enactment as a full eleven months away renders curious the need for such haste in distributing the edict (3:15). One might consider the effect that this delay will have on the Jewish population. After hearing the edict read to them, they will have almost a full year to wait in dread anticipation. In one sense, the delay is almost as cruel as the act itself. The psychological damage of requiring the people to live for an extended period in such anxiety, expecting such terror, would be great. In another sense, though, the delay is a measure of generosity on the part of Haman. The eleven-month period would allow people ample time to make an escape from Persian territory or at the very least to locate a secure place to hide during that one day. That Haman is so stupid not to think of this possibility is inconsistent with his characterization elsewhere in the story. Perhaps Haman, like a taunting bully who never actually throws a punch, is really banking on the psychological more than the physical aspect of this punishment, to make people afraid and to disrupt their lives completely.

The result of the decree's dissemination differs (3:15).There is a juxtaposition between the response inside and outside the palace, that of Haman and the king and that of the rest of the population. The reader is provided with a split point of view, being able to see both locales at the same time. That Ahasuerus and Haman do not just drink but "sat down to drink" suggests that their imbibing is not merely a celebratory toast, but a lengthy drinking event. Their drinking represents a solidification of their relationship, a recognition of each other as compatriots, as "insiders" (Beal 1999, 56). The relaxation of the two contrasts starkly with the brewing pandemonium in the streets, where the entire city of Susa is confused and dismayed. The Hebrew verb *bûk*, "thrown into confusion," appears only two other times in the Hebrew Bible; it is also used to describe the Israelites wandering aimlessly in the desert (Exod 14:3) and cattle groaningly wandering about without pasture (Joel 1:18). This term, therefore, suggests not only the city's confusion and agitation, but also their sense of feeling lost, forlorn, and helpless. Noteworthy is the detail that not only the Jews but also all people, the entire city, are disturbed by the new decree. The news is troubling to would-be assassins and would-be victims alike. Clearly not everyone in Susa despises Jews as Haman does.

Theological and Ethical Analysis

Standing at this point in history, one cannot read this episode without hearing echoes of the Shoah. Haman's "final solution" to "the Jewish problem" sounds chillingly familiar. The book of Esther is surprisingly prophetic about the anti-Judaism that would later come. Haman's edict is a full-scale case of genocide and, as such, can reflect more broadly any situation in which people are catalogued for harm because of their ethnic identity or any circumstance of "ethnic cleansing." Racial hostility, in its most fundamental sense, occurs when the differences between peoples are stressed over the commonalities. Any such perceived difference or otherness, by its very nature, is treated as dangerous and hostile to the culture in power. In Haman's argument, the linchpin he chooses is the difference of the Jews (3:8). The attitude that he promulgates includes projecting one group as anomalous but everyone else as homogenous, presenting a deviant "them" versus a unified "us" (Beal 1999, 51-52). Racial hatred includes generalizing an entire group from the actions and character of a lone individual, assuming that "they're all like that" (3:6). The result of Haman's actions affects not only the Jews, but also the whole kingdom; his bigotry leads, in the end, to a crisis of state. It is an example of how discrimination does not just affect the group in question; instead, everyone is affected negatively when one people experiences discrimination. The whole society suffers adversely in some way from such prejudices. Prejudice can exist either in the form of the blatant animosity of Haman or the unwitting indifference of Ahasuerus; in the end it does not matter, for the result is the same.

Various other ethical concerns are raised by the episode. First, the story illustrates the dangers of vindictiveness and greed. Haman's vengefulness stems from feelings of being slighted and from thinking that he is not given his proper due. Yet how quickly the power struggle escalates after he decides to act on his vindictiveness. The edict would also not have been approved if Ahasuerus, the wealthy king who succumbs to the temptation to have even more, were not so greedy. Second, the Jews cannot be identified by outward appearance; in other words, they can "pass" in Persian society. As Clines observes, the book as a whole presents a mixed message vis-à-vis Jewish identity, for "the Jewish people find themselves under a death sentence because one Jew acts like a Jew and tells his people he is a Jew; they escape through the good offices of another Jew who has pretended she is not a Jew" (1990, 48). In such situations of discrimination, should one keep quiet like Esther or speak up like Mordecai; is it wiser to blend in or to stand out? Third is the question of a personal code of ethics, represented by the predicaments of Mordecai and Vashti. They represent the cusp of a dilemma: should an individual stand up for her or his principles if doing so will result in harm to others? This is not to suggest that either Vashti or Mordecai can be expected to anticipate the ramifications of their decisions. Yet both characters manifest that place where individual morality intersects with the welfare of many. In addition, the fact that Mordecai's and Vashti's situations run in parallel lines gives the sense that all the dangers of racism (Mordecai's problem) stated above are not unique to it, but are parallel to the dangers of sexism (Vashti's problem). Indeed, the lines blur between the two, resulting in a kind of "feminization" of Mordecai and a "Judaization" of Vashti (Beal 1997, 47).

The timing of the events hints, very subtly, at Jewish tradition. The month in which Haman has lots cast, Nisan, is the month of the Passover celebration (cf. Exod 12:2-3; Lev 23:5; Deut 16:1 [in the last, the month is referred to as Abib, its name in Israel's calendar]). There is, of course, no suggestion in the story that the Jews are observing the festivals. Yet the very month recalls the theological concept of redemption, and Levenson sees this fact as a prediction that it is redemption, and not fate, that will triumph (1997, 70). A further similarity is evidenced in Moses' character as an in-between figure (Beal 1999, 49). In the exodus story, Moses is able to succeed against Pharaoh precisely because he lives between the Egyptian and the Hebrew worlds. Esther, another liminal figure, living in between the Persian and the Jewish worlds, will likewise be able to succeed against her Pharaohs, in the words of the Passover haggadah, because she understands how to act in both cultures. Yet the similarity with the exodus story also highlights a difference, a divine hole. In the account of the bringing out the Hebrews from Egypt, it is their God YHWH who is the hero; redemption comes ultimately because of divine concern and not human effort. In the story of Esther, however, there is no God hearing the cries of the oppressed (Exod 3:7-10). Redemption falls to strictly human instrumentality. In the world of this story, the only command(ment)s, the only *miṣwōt,* are from the king and the government—not from the deity.

ESTHER AND MORDECAI'S CONVERSATION (4:1-17)

This episode follows immediately upon the conclusion of the previous episode, providing a more specific illustration of the confusion in the city, especially the distress of the Jewish population. Esther learns of Mordecai's mourning and initiates a conversation with him. At Mordecai's urging, she decides to attempt to resolve the present crisis.

Literary Analysis

No longer in the realms of extravagant drink or fancy cosmetics, as the episode begins, the visual imagery turns sober. Coarse sackcloth replaces fine bleached linen (1:6). The focus lies fully upon the two protagonists Mordecai and Esther, recording their responses to Haman's decree about the planned destruction of the Jewish people. Mordecai's grief, along with that of the Jewish community as a whole, is presented first (vv. 1-3). Responsive actions on his part both open (v. 1) and close (v. 17) the episode. At verse 4, Esther is brought back into the picture, and the first part of the scene is presented from her point of view (Fox 2001, 60). She will continue at the center of action through the next episode as well. When, at the end, Esther charges Mordecai and the Jews in Susa to fast, the first reversal of this story transpires. Mordecai comes to command Esther (v. 8), but in the end it is instead Esther who is commanding him (vv. 16-17).

The first instances of direct speech of both Mordecai and Esther occur here. Their utterances have been reported only indirectly up until this point (2:10, 15, 20, 22; 3:4). As this is the sole point in the entire story when Mordecai speaks, the narrative characterizes him as essentially taciturn, while Esther, in contrast, will prove to be quite loquacious. The dialogue is suspenseful and terse, with the repetition of the phrase "such a time as this" (v. 14) providing a sense of the urgency of the present crisis. The scene follows a sequence of straight narration (v. 4), indirect discourse with detailed narrative transitions (vv. 5-9), and finally direct discourse with minimal narrative transitions (vv. 10-17) (Bush 1996, 392-93). Descriptions of the servants' actions of relaying the messages back and forth become briefer as the episode continues, until Esther and Mordecai seem to be speaking directly in their final statements; this characteristic makes the conversation seem more immediate and the pace of the narrative accelerate as it proceeds through the episode. The narrative pace, however, does not match the pace of the actions described, for it most likely would take considerable time, possibly several hours, between the sending and the receiving of any given message.

Space plays an important role in the episode. Three levels of space are evident: (1) outside the gate, (2) inside the palace generally, and (3) inside the inner court. One of the story's protagonists resides in each of these levels. Mordecai is in the first area, "the open square of the city in front of the king's gate" (v. 6). This is fully public space, open to all. Esther is in the second area, inside the palace. The narrative stresses the spatial separation between the two relatives. The eunuch Hathach and the other servants are intermediaries between these two levels, between inside and outside, liminal figures transversing these two areas while Mordecai and Esther are unable or unwilling to do so. Ahasuerus inhabits, and controls, the third area, the inner court. The parallel phrases "to the king" and "to the inner court" (more clearly parallel in the Hebrew) equate this level of space explicitly with the king; it is his exclusive domain (v. 11). Clearly, these three levels of space reflect varying degrees of power: the king is at the center, holding the power of life and death; Esther lies in the next level of power, not in control, but in proximity to the king and having some degree of influence over him; and Mordecai is physically the farthest away from the inner realm and from the center of power.

Exegetical Analysis

The narrative first reports how distressed Mordecai is at the situation (v. 1). Both the visible ("sackcloth and ashes") and the audible ("wailing with a loud and bitter cry") reflect his mood; that is, he makes apparent to all his emotional state through sight and sound. The sackcloth and ashes, along with the fasting at the end of this scene (v. 16), are typical ancient expressions of grief and despair. Sackcloth and ashes are often used in the Hebrew Bible when people lament and mourn because of death, in anticipation of destruction, or as a sign of penitence (e.g., 2 Sam 3:31; Jer 6:26). Fasting is often used in conjunction both with sackcloth and ashes (e.g., Jonah 3:6; Isa 58:5) and with prayer (e.g., Ezra 8:21-23; Dan 9:3).

Transversing the city, Mordecai goes up to the gate of the palace (v. 2). Why, the reader is not sure. To express his dismay to palace officials, presumably inside? To record an official protest? To plead for amnesty? As one might imagine a camera panning back, in the next verse the narrative reveals that Mordecai is not alone, for all the Jews in the kingdom are seen responding in precisely the same manner (v. 3). Mordecai's behavior is shown, therefore, to be characteristic. He is a representative Jew, just as Haman earlier considered him to be when deciding to kill all those whom Mordecai represents (3:6; note also how this status continues at 5:13; 6:10; 9:29; 10:3). The Jews do not attempt to hide or blend in to general Persian society but make a very public display; everyone will know who is Jewish. Perhaps the non-Jews, seeing the distress of their fellow citizens, begin to develop the sympathy for the Jews that will become evident later (8:17).

Esther responds by taking up this same distress (v. 4). She feels herself to be in solidarity with the Jews—if they are upset, she will be upset as well. The surprising thing about Esther's response is that she becomes disturbed even before knowing *why*. Her sympathy with the Jewish plight appears to be great, for merely knowing that they are agitated makes her so as well. The Hebrew term that is translated "deeply distressed" (the verb *ḥûl*) can refer to whirling, dancing, or writhing in anxiety. The use of this term to describe Esther's state of being suggests not only inner mental anguish but also movement and physical pain. Her physical as well as mental writhing mirrors Mordecai's wandering throughout the city in grief. This scene, at its outset, reflects the two characters acting in concert, simultaneously pacing about to express their grief and dismay.

Also surprising is that Esther does not know what is happening in the greater kingdom. She must hear of her cousin's situation only indirectly, through the servants who presumably travel outside the palace more freely than she is able to do (v. 4). That she is unaware of the news shows how clearly this decree is intended only for those outside the palace; Esther, like others inside the palace, is not expected to be affected by the happenings. The dichotomy between inside and outside, at the conclusion of the last episode, continues (3:15). Even if one might suggest that Esther is not told of the edict because no one knows that she is Jewish, as a (presumed) non-Jew she would still have been expected to attack any Jews if the decree is intended to apply to those inside the palace. Esther's lack of knowledge makes it clear that the information and subsequent confusion is not inside the palace but only outside it, in the city and provinces. She lives in a protected universe.

Esther follows a typical human pattern of response to a catastrophic situation—first she mourns, and then she pulls herself together to figure out what to do about the problem. Unlike Mordecai and the rest of the Jews, she is not content to stay in a constant state of lamentation; she moves beyond the loss to positive action, acting concretely to send clothing to Mordecai. Parallel phrases in the Hebrew make it clear that Esther wants to do two things: "to clothe Mordecai" and "to take away his sackcloth from upon him" (author's translation). She is attempting to care for him. One sees in this instance the beginning of Esther's trait of mothering both Mordecai and the greater Jewish community that will continue throughout the story (Kirk-Duggan 1999). As the text notes how Mordecai is prevented from entering the palace because of his attire (v. 2), one expects that Esther is providing him the proper clothing so that he would be permitted inside the king's compound, perhaps so that she might talk to him or that she might try to comfort him. Esther seemingly wants to be with Mordecai face-to-face.

Mordecai, however, rebuffs her actions. The narrative reports his response, in two curt words in Hebrew, as "but he did not receive" (author's translation). Just as when Mordecai refused to bow to Haman (3:2), he does not explain why he refuses Esther's gift. Again, the reader sees Mordecai's stubbornness come to the fore; not putting on the clothes so he could enter the palace makes things more difficult for everyone. He obeys the queen no more than he obeys the king. And as before, he does not concern himself with any possible ramifications of his noncompliance.

When her initial response (sending clothing) proves unsuccessful, Esther tries another tactic. Instead of dealing with Mordecai directly, she employs an intermediary, her servant Hathach. Her choice to ask for information through the servant does meet with success. She initiates the conversation that comprises the remainder of this scene. Esther shows herself to be curious, desiring the information that has apparently been denied her in the palace; she wants to know "what was happening and why" (v. 5).

What Hathach learns from Mordecai is "all that had happened to him, and the exact sum of money that Haman had promised to pay into the king's treasuries for the destruction of the Jews" (v. 7). All that happened *to Mordecai* is a rather odd concept, for at this point nothing has happened "to him." Even the anticipated future event of violence will happen equally to all Jews and not to him alone. Perhaps instead Mordecai is referring to the earlier event of his own refusal to bow at his colleagues' urgings (3:2-6), though that action is more removed and hence less likely. The language of the narrative renders Mordecai as rather self-centered, especially as the egocentric Haman presents his experiences in the same way (6:13). He sees himself as a victim, when actually he was (to a greater or lesser degree) a contributor to the troubling situation (cf. Edwards 1990). Mordecai also knows details about the arrangement, that Haman bought off the king, and even the exact amount of money that changed hands. His inclusion of this information to Esther may be so that the enormity of the bribe will give her a sense of Haman's animosity. Does this information signify that the bribe, which had been related as though it occurred behind closed doors (3:8-11, 15), is common knowledge among the general Persian populace; that is, all the people know not only the text of the decree as it was read to them (3:14), but also how it came about? And if so, do they also know Mordecai's role in the decision? Or instead, has Mordecai alone come to this information, as he has come upon other information in the past (2:22)? If so, he more fully emerges in this scene as an individual who has an ear to the ground, who knows what there is to know.

How Mordecai is able to obtain a copy of the decree is also not reported (v. 8), for it was only to be disseminated to the general public by oral proclamation, and no mention is made of its being posted for all to read (3:13-14). If he himself received a copy, it would give further weight to the possibility that Mordecai is some sort of lower official in the Persian regime (3:2-3). He also clearly appears to be a leader in the Jewish community, as he is later in a position to command them (v. 16). The copy he sends is a physical counterpart to the clothes that Esther has sent (Clines 1984a, 35). That Mordecai forwards a written document to inform Esther also suggests that she is literate, as upper class and royal women increasingly became in Hellenistic times (Ilan 1995, 191-94; Crenshaw 1998, 47-49).

Verse 8b more literally reads "to show to Esther and to tell her, and to charge her to enter to the king to implore favor of him, and to seek before him" (author's translation). Each of these three actions has been significant in the narrative up to this point (Beal 1999, 62-63). Mordecai wants Hathach merely to "tell" or "report to" Esther. Esther's intelligence is assumed, that if she is just given the proper information, she will understand it and its ramifications. Hathach's *showing* her and *telling* her continues the theme of a sensory visible and audible response initiated earlier in this episode (v. 1). What Mordecai urges Esther to do is to seek the king's favor, and his suggestion is based upon past experience: the manner by which Esther succeeded earlier in the palace was explicitly through winning others' favor (2:9, 15, 17). Mordecai anticipates—correctly—that this is how Esther will succeed again. Moreover, that Esther is to seek favor "before him" recognizes again how everything in this environment must be accomplished in the king's presence.

The next section records the subsequent conversation between Esther and Mordecai, after she has been apprised of the problematic recent events, with each individual responding and servants scurrying back and forth to relay the replies (vv. 9-17). It is conversation at a distance on a variety of levels; space, status, and sexual difference separate the two characters (Beal 1997, 71). Esther reports to Mordecai that if she were to go to the king on her own accord, she would be subject to death (v. 11). That she has not been called to the king for some time does not bode well for any hope that she would receive amnesty from Ahasuerus. Though Esther has been in the court for several years, she still feels her situation to be precarious. This statement may be read as a protest against Mordecai's suggestion, giving the reason she does not want to follow it (v. 8). More likely, Esther is merely telling what the situation looks like inside the palace, just as Mordecai had informed her of the view outside the palace. She may be recalling that when Vashti's fate was in Ahasuerus's hands, he was not charitable. Esther cannot necessarily expect that he will be gracious to her either, to choose to extend to her the sceptre and, consequently, life. She would risk not only her royal position, like Vashti, but also her very existence (Levenson 1997, 80). As Mordecai possibly does not know palace customs about entering the palace gate in mourning costume (vv. 2, 4), she explains to him palace regulations about going before the king, something of which she is not sure he is aware. Esther's comment that everyone knows of this custom seems to chide Mordecai; along with the custom about entering in sackcloth, both customs are presented in a way that sounds as though they are common knowledge among government employees ("all the king's servants") and also broadly among all Persian civilians ("[all] the people of the king's provinces"; v. 11). Mordecai's grief and distress keep him from thinking with a clear head, causing him to forget things he (most likely) knows, or at least preventing him from thinking through the situation clearly. Both Mordecai and Vashti before him tend to respond rashly, without thinking through the consequence of their disobedience, when refusing to bow (3:2-4) and refusing to come to Ahasuerus's party (1:12) without stated reasons. In contrast, Esther weighs the ramifications of acting out the disobedience Mordecai impulsively suggests.

Mordecai replies that Esther should not consider herself immune to the danger, that if she does not act the Jews will still be saved, and that circumstances may have brought her to queenship for a purpose (vv. 13-14). Mordecai's advice to Esther has shifted dramatically with this turn of events. Previously, he had counseled her unequivocally *not* to speak of her ancestry (2:10, 20). Now, however, he is urging her to do that very thing, insisting that she *must* speak. Failure to speak about her people would be her downfall.

A closer examination of Mordecai's advice is in order. He warns Esther that "you and your father's family will perish" (v. 14). Esther is an orphan, with father and mother dead (2:7). The narrative does not report that any other more distant relatives are still alive and indeed gives the impression that this is why Mordecai has taken her on, that he is the only (or at least the primary) close kin left to Esther. He is a paternal relative, from the lineage of Esther's birth father, Abihail, and is now acting directly as her father (2:15). Therefore, Esther's "father's family" *is* Mordecai. In the way in which he words this statement, Mordecai is euphemistically revealing concern for his own skin as well as for Esther's. If he truly believes what he says—that if Esther does not do anything, all will be saved except her family—then Mordecai urges Esther for selfish reasons as well as for her safety. He is willing to put her at danger for his own safety.

According to Mordecai's logic, there are three possible results. (1) If Esther does not approach the king, she and her father's family will be killed but all the other Jews saved. (2) If Esther approaches the king and is not successful, she will die (according to the king's law about approaching unsummoned) and presumably all the Jews will risk death (according to Haman's decree). (3) If Esther approaches the king and is successful, all Jews will live. Therefore, Mordecai is really asking Esther to take the risk of going before the king unsummoned on behalf of herself and himself (her "father's family"). If she does nothing at all, all the Jews will live, through the alternative deliverance he anticipates, but the two of them will die. But if she fails, all the Jews will die. Mordecai is therefore expressing a willingness to risk all of the Jews' lives for his own (and Esther's) life.

Scholars debate whether Mordecai's reference to deliverance arising "from another quarter" represents a veiled allusion to God

(v. 14). The term *māqōm*, "place" or "quarter," is used in the Talmudic tradition as an epithet for God. Some interpreters argue that Mordecai's statement alludes to God acting "behind the scene" (e.g., Moore 1971, 52; Levenson 1997, 81; Crawford 1999, 905; Berlin 2001a, 44). Other interpreters maintain that one cannot unequivocally read an allusion to God here (e.g., Fox 2001, 63; Bush 1996, 396). A further option is that Mordecai, an individual who seems to know what there is to know in Susa, may be hinting at a political coup in response to Haman's edict. If one takes Mordecai's statement to refer to God's involvement, then the fact that Esther does act would signify that God does not play a role in the Jews' ultimate redemption, that Esther's success follows solely from her human efforts. Because Esther does not "keep silence" and chooses to help the Jews, this "other place" is never needed, so ultimately the reader will never know what it represents.

Esther's reply is recorded in verse 16; she requests that all the Jews observe a three-day fast, along with her and her female servants, and notifies Mordecai that then she will approach King Ahasuerus. If one understands her first response as explanatory (v. 11), this statement does not so much reflect a change of mind on Esther's part (i.e., that Mordecai has convinced her), but shows her making plans as to the manner in which she will proceed. This is the first time the reader sees Esther herself as part of Jewish society; up to this point she has been one step removed, connected to Mordecai who has been connected to the Jewish community. And, of course, she has been actively hiding her Jewishness from palace personnel. But now she is claiming these people as her own. Their actions influence her, as her actions will later influence them when she pleads their case before Ahasuerus.

Esther requests the Jews to change their method of fasting; instead of haphazardly fasting as a response to the news of impending disaster (v. 3), they are told to hold a specified fast "on [her] behalf." The actual reasons for asking the Jews to fast, though, are not clear. Does she desire fasting to impress an (unmentioned) God? To provide her moral courage? To buy her time? To give her a clear head, unfettered by all the royal wine, with which to strategize? Perhaps her motives are not for herself but for the Jewish people as a whole. The common enterprise of fasting together would result in forming them into a stronger and more unified community and would have them do something more optimistic and purposeful than their current wailing and lamenting (v. 3). As in any situation of fear and uncertainty, performing a constructive action here gives the Jews the precious commodities of hope and utility, the sense that they are doing something constructive that might make a difference to their new spokeswoman's success.

In her acquiescence, Esther's language includes a subtle refutation of Mordecai's logic. Whereas Mordecai threatens that she will die if not choosing to help the Jews, Esther repeats Mordecai's language ("perish") but twists his thought, instead anticipating death if she *does* help the Jews. The Hebrew text of Esther's final clause allows it to be read as either temporal or conditional. Esther may be saying either "when I perish, I perish" or "if I perish, I perish." If she intends the former, Esther is already accepting her death as a foregone conclusion; if the latter, she is holding out some hope that the result may not be that dire. In any event, it is clear that Esther expresses a willingness to be martyred for the sake of others.

In the space of this scene, Esther progresses into a commanding figure right before the reader's eyes. At the beginning, Esther's first reaction is to attempt to help Mordecai (v. 4). As his queen, she would have had the authority to command him to do what she desires, to remove his mourning clothing so he could come through the palace gate, but she does not do so. Esther has no problem, however, in commanding Hathach (v. 5). After all these years in the palace environment, an environment teeming with servants (1:10; 2:2, 9, 13; 3:3, 12, 15; 4:4, and later 6:3, 5, 14; 7:8, 10; 8:9, 10, 14), Esther has necessarily become accustomed to ordering about palace servants. Yet at verse 8, when Mordecai attempts to command Esther, she does not unquestionably acquiesce as she did when she was younger (2:10, 20). Mordecai changes his tactics; when he next speaks, his language has an explanatory tone, attempting to convince rather than require (v.

13). At the point of the narrative introduction to Esther's final statement, the two appear to converse on equal footing. "And Esther said to reply to Mordecai" (v. 15) precisely parallels the wording of the introduction to Mordecai's statement, "And Mordecai said to reply to Esther" (v. 13; author's translations). At the conclusion of the conversation, Esther acts in a fully imperial manner. Her final statement includes a string of imperatives: go, gather, fast, do not eat, do not drink (v. 16). Implicitly, as well, she will command her servants in their fasting. Esther and Mordecai have shifted places. Instead of his trying to command her, she now commands him—and he obeys fully and without question (v. 17). Her relationship with her foster father has changed. During this scene, Esther's persona shifts to that of a commanding presence in the kingdom.

Servants play an important role in this episode, for they are the ones who make the exchange between Mordecai and Esther possible. They continually shuttle back and forth, between the palace interior and outside the palace gate. First Hathach is commissioned to Mordecai (vv. 5-6), then back to Esther (vv. 7-9), then back to Mordecai (v. 10). Oddly enough, though, at verse 12 the text switches to the plural, "*they* told Mordecai" (italics mine). (The plural "them" of the NRSV, in verse 13, is not present in the Hebrew.) This change gives the impression that perhaps not only a single servant, Hathach, is active as a courier, but also others are pressed into service (perhaps the female servants and eunuchs of v. 4?). After verse 12, the reader is to continue to imagine the conversation continuing via courier, though any messengers are not explicitly mentioned again. After all of these interchanges, Hathach and any other servants conveying Esther and Mordecai's messages clearly know Esther's ethnic identity. And they keep her secret well. Indeed, the fate of the Jews rides upon the accuracy and the loyalty of Hathach and the others. Hathach, especially, would find himself in a difficult place. He is in actuality the king's servant, not Esther's; he has merely been appointed to tend to her (v. 5). One would expect, therefore, that he would feel primary loyalty to Ahasuerus. Instead, he favors Esther, in that he chooses not to make known her secret. His decision, like that of Esther, is one of life and death. The legislation for the Jews' destruction is a royal edict (3:12); circumventing this edict, as Hathach does, involves going against the king. And in this kingdom, traitors are killed for their disloyalty (2:23).

Nor are Esther and Mordecai fully loyal and obedient. They both display some doubt as to the certainty of royal law, by not treating Persian royal edicts as inviolable as they are supposed to be (8:8). Mordecai thinks that Ahasuerus's mind may be changed, and even if it is not, that the edict may somehow be circumvented (v. 14). Esther may think that it is not certain that Ahasuerus will kill her for coming into the inner court without a royal summons (v. 16). Both of these perspectives show that the king's lock on the obedience of his subjects is not airtight. A crack is opened, even before the reader knows the outcome of the events. That his subjects are even *thinking* that a monarch's decree may be circumvented depicts a king who does not have the full obedience and cooperation he imagines.

The fasting in this episode contrasts with the theme of feasting and drinking running throughout the book of Esther. In this environment of constant drink, the mere decision *not* to drink stands out. Sometimes the desire to show that one disagrees with a political administration involves not outright insurrection, but simply making it publicly obvious that one does not value those things that the administration values. The fasting, therefore, functions symbolically in the story an act of resistance; such refraining from drink may even be seen as a form of nonviolent protest. That this protest occurs not only in the Jewish quarters of the city, but in the palace itself, under the king's nose, renders it even more dangerous. Just as Hathach and any other couriers, Esther's female servants (if they agree to do as Esther anticipates they will; v. 16) are choosing whether to support the king or the queen. Their fasting makes visible where their loyalty lies, and, as individuals low in the hierarchy of power, their decision is a risky action in and of itself.

This episode represents a juncture for the character of Esther. Up until this point she has not appeared as a truly full character; she has been passive, pliant, silent, and more spoken about than speaking herself. She has accommodated herself toward all the men in her life: Mordecai, Hegai, Ahasuerus. But now, some five years after being made queen, Esther has grown up. She no longer obeys unquestioningly. Moreover, Esther comes out of her silence. Previously she was known as the one who did not speak (2:10, 20) and did not ask (2:15). Now she speaks up—and after this point she becomes quite verbal.

What will be required of her are no longer the duties of a child. In the present crisis, Esther is now faced with adult responsibilities. "Such a time as this" turns into Esther's opportunity to become her own person (van Wijk-Bos 1998, 129). Even before attempting to approach the king, she demonstrates great courage. For obedient, pleasant Esther, it is a great step to say that she will do something against decree. In an environment so ruled by law, such an act is not only terribly risky, but also countercultural. Esther must realize that she will need to adapt. The novelty of a new queen has worn off; Esther must get Ahasuerus's attention by surprising him, by relating to him in a fresh and unexpected fashion. Faced with the challenge of working from the position of one who is no longer popular and naturally advantaged, she will have to make the system work to bring her back to a place of advantage. No longer having the king's attention as the sexiest young thing in the palace, Esther will have to figure out new tactics to succeed, tactics that no longer include physical attractiveness as a primary component. By the conclusion of the episode, the situation of chapter 2 is turned upside down: no longer hiding, Esther elects to reveal; and Esther, not Mordecai, is the one in charge.

Various parts of Esther's identity begin to emerge and converge. Since arriving at the palace, Esther has been living out of her identity as a Persian in the court. The Jewish identity she left behind in silence now needs to be integrated with her position as Persian queen. At the beginning of the episode, her lack of sackcloth signifies her distance from the Jewish community; "she is in the realm of no sackcloth when sackcloth is the fashion of the day for the Jews of Persia" (Beal 1999, 60). By the conclusion, however, she has fully acknowledged her people, beginning to act as their national leader. Esther's growth requires her to endorse the part of her identity that has remained dormant during these years. Her new abilities to integrate, as will play out during the remainder of the story, demonstrate her growing maturity. Another part of Esther's identity is that of a woman in a male realm. She is reconstituting her female roles. Now she begins to learn how not to be the "good daughter"; next, she will learn how not to be the "good wife." This episode is the second time in the story, after Vashti's drinking party (1:9), when women join together from the community at large (v. 16). Does Esther find in this group a nascent feminist solidarity? Perhaps she recognizes the potential of a collaborative women's community in which her female servants no longer merely cater to her but also are her allies. This previously male-oriented young girl is finding strength from the support of a group of women.

Theological and Ethical Analysis

More clearly than any other place in the book, this episode highlights the power of the human spirit in the face of adversity. The characters reflect the ability to move beyond grief and rise to the occasion with which they are faced. Recognition is given to the cathartic aspect of grieving as they take essential time in sackcloth. But at some point in the grieving process it is necessary to move beyond despair toward action. The Jews demonstrate that oftentimes the best medicine for an anxious heart is to go out and do whatever one can see to do. Hope can arise and healing can begin through the very deed of action itself.

Decisions must be made; loyalties are tested. Crisis situations often bring persons to decisions they otherwise would not have reason to make. And in the process of making such choices, identity is forged and allegiances more clearly drawn. Esther chooses to side with her Jewish kindred over against the court; the servants choose to side with the queen over against the king. In such crisis situations, questions of identity emerge as one often discovers who one really is. The characters—especially Esther—recover their identity through solidarity with others.

It is both communal destiny—that of the Jewish population— and an individual sense of destiny that the episode reflects. Esther stands at a fork in her personal journey; she is faced with a difficult choice about which path to follow. Certainly the temptation to do nothing would be strong for a person in her position. Life has been generous and pleasant, and the threat is distant and uncertain: why make a fuss? It requires personal courage to decide to stand out, to take the more treacherous road. For those whose personalities and identities are still in the process of formation, like the young Esther, facing a crisis head-on brings a greater emotional maturity. Her decision to stand against injustice represents the sense of honor and community responsibility that Esther begins to feel. As in any battle, the honorable death is to go out fighting rather than be caught in retreat. At such decisive points in life, one is faced with the choice of being remembered as a person who remained silent in the face of danger and injustice, or a person who heroically chose to speak out against it. In essence, this is an existential concern, the need to make sense of one's existence. What is my purpose, my reason for living? It is this sense of purpose that Mordecai advocates, suggesting a higher aspiration for Esther's life than she is currently living out. There are times when a situation is such that it calls persons out of complacency into action. Indeed, the action itself is what is required rather than the outcome, the sense that injustice must be opposed no matter the personal cost. It is this type of action that Esther chooses to take.

A theological question arises from the Jews' activities of donning sackcloth and fasting that initiate and conclude the episode (vv. 1-3, 16). Are they to be understood as religious activities? Throughout the Hebrew Bible, wearing sackcloth and ashes and fasting are often explicitly presented as religious activities. Yet an observant reader will note that the text of the book of Esther could easily have signified a hope to influence God to action as the reason for the Jews' behavior, as is the case elsewhere when prayer and petitions to God accompany these activities (e.g., Ezra 8:21-23; Dan 9:3). Here, in contrast, there is no mention of corresponding prayer. As wearing sackcloth and putting ashes upon one's body are typical ways to express grief in the ancient world, perhaps the Jews are merely acting out their anguish. The absence of any reference to God in the narrative at this point, especially in light of earlier biblical traditions that include God, is telling.

More than overt religiosity or God-talk, fate is the significant theme in the episode. Just as Haman had left to chance the date of the Jews' destruction (3:7), so here both Mordecai and Esther speak in the language of chance and fate. When ruminating upon Esther's ascendancy to the throne, Mordecai comments, "Who knows? Perhaps you have come to royal dignity for just such a time as this" (v. 14). He tosses things to destiny, suggesting that it is fate that brought Esther to queenship to answer the present need. Other biblical figures who use similar language, asking "who knows?" about future events, do so explicitly within a consideration of God's role in those events (2 Sam 12:22; Jonah 3:9; Joel 2:14). It is therefore highly significant that Mordecai does not use this language. Esther herself also throws things to the fates with her reply, "and if I perish, I perish" (v. 16). With her and others' fasting, she does all in her power to bring about success; after that, it is up to chance whether she succeeds or fails. Life and death hang not on the deity, but on fate. The episode represents how human beings often are placed in the position of acting without knowing God's desires, with no certainty that God will bring about success for them. Lacking the obvious presence and intervention of God, one throws the dice without a clue as to how they will land; one leaves the outcome to fate. In making her decision to act in the face of great uncertainty about the result, Esther reflects the truest sense of personal courage.

In all, the episode exhibits a delicious ambiguity with regard to God's presence in the events. As Berlin observes, "God is most present and most absent in this chapter" (2001a, 44). Yet God is neither fully present nor fully absent. The narrative represents an in-between perspective, the juncture between faith and agnosticism. It is a hallmark of good literature to leave room for the reader's imagination, to avoid filling in every gap. In the end, the story reminds its readers that one should not fret about resolving the issue of divine involvement—either in the events of the story or in the events of one's own life—but leave the question in the realm of ambiguity. As Mordecai says, who knows?

ESTHER APPROACHES AND HOSTS (5:1-8)

This episode follows immediately upon the conclusion of
Esther's fasting. Beginning "on the third day," it cuts her involvement in the general three-day fast a bit short. Preparing herself,
Esther enters the king's inner court. In reply to Ahasuerus's queries
about what she wants, she invites him and Haman to a first, and
then a second, drinking party. The episode resolves a question
from the previous episode (will Esther die?) but creates another
question (when will she request reprieve from Haman's edict?).

Literary Analysis

As this episode commences, the tension is thick enough to be cut
with a knife when Esther risks her life with this simple action. Yet
the narrative is sparse, leaving it solely to the reader to recognize the
suspense. The scene is introduced by a description of the physical
environment before the primary action begins, much like a photo-
graphic snapshot or a still life painting (v. 1). There is precise
description of the space, of the physical placement of items; the
inner court, king's palace, king's hall, palace entrance, and throne
area are all noted. Where they are located in relation to one another is provided with greater detail than is typical in biblical narrative. In this spatial view, one sees the inner court running parallel
to the king's hall, then through the hall to the entrance where the
king sits on the throne. Contrast is also provided between Esther's
standing and Ahasuerus's sitting. That the narrator takes such great
pains to describe the physical scene gives the impression that it is
vital for the reader to be able to imagine precisely what the setting
looks like.

The initial description is from Esther's perspective. The reader
looks through her eyes as she stands in the inner court and can see
"the king ... sitting on his royal throne inside the palace" (v. 1*b*).
At verse 2 the point of view shifts, and the reader is now on the
throne with Ahasuerus when he looks up and "[sees] Queen
Esther standing in the court." This is repeated information, for the
fact of Esther's standing has already been reported, from a neutral
point of view, in verse 1. Ahasuerus extends the sceptre to Esther,

toward which she approaches and then touches. All of this action has proceeded in silence; not a word has been uttered or a sound heard. The silence is broken only when the king speaks, beginning the dialogue between them that comprises the remainder of the episode, first in the throne area and then at the drinking party to which Esther invites Ahasuerus and Haman. The episode concludes with another reversal. Esther has been in the habit of "going in" to Ahasuerus and his environment, first when she was gathered along with the other young women (2:8), then when she went in to the king for evaluation (2:16), and most recently here at verse 2. Now the tables are turned, as Ahasuerus comes in to Esther's presence and physical environment (v. 5).

The focus in the episode is upon the protagonists Esther and Ahasuerus. Haman, though present at the party, is not an active character, but for the first time he and the queen appear together. Notably, however, Ahasuerus is not once indicated by his proper name; he is only referred to generically as "the king." The narrative tends to indicate Esther, in contrast, by proper name at every possible opportunity. Her name, "Esther," is repeated nine times in this brief section. This repetition, along with the king's namelessness, makes Esther appear to have greater personality and individuality than does he. Though both are on stage, the spotlight falls predominantly upon her.

Exegetical Analysis

A strong sense of royalty pervades this episode. Various noun forms of the Hebrew root *mālak,* "to rule," appear twenty-one times throughout these eight verses. These terms refer to the king, the queen, the palace, the throne, and the kingdom. (This repetition is not as evident in translation, as English uses a greater variety of terms for these concepts.) Such redundancy provides atmospheric description, as the royal aspect almost overwhelms. This characteristic is especially evident in verse 1, which includes six instances of forms of *mālak.* Portions of the palace are mentioned twice in quick succession, "and she stood in the inner court of the house of the king, in front of the house of the king," and then for a third time (albeit with a bit different terminology as "the house of royalty") as the verse concludes (author's translations). The reader begins this episode with a sense of awe, a sense of how official the environment of the queen and king's encounter will be.

The narrative notes how Esther "puts on royalty" (author's translation). This phrase is not a fashion statement or a comment specifically about luxurious clothing. It is literally *malkût,* "royalty," that Esther wears. (The Hebrew verb *lābas̆,* "to clothe," occurs elsewhere in the Hebrew Bible with abstract concepts, as it does here with the abstract concept of royalty, as well as with actual clothing. Esther's donning royalty must be distinguished from Mordecai's later action of wearing actual "royal garments," where the terminology differs [6:8; 8:15].) In preparation for her anticipated meeting with the king, Esther girds herself with all the power and authority she can muster. This view of Esther is considerably different from the one by which she was initially introduced. What she wore then, most likely suggested by Hegai and not chosen by herself, was probably some sort of attire selected to highlight her physical attractiveness. Now, however, sporting a pretty face and figure is no longer her concern; instead she wears an aura of political authority. Esther has grown into her position of queen. No longer the "girl" she was in chapter 2, the primary characteristic about Esther at this point in the story is her queenly demeanor. It is an inner quality, the "royalty" that she finds for herself. Even though Ahasuerus is in a more powerful position than she, the person sitting on the throne who makes the decisions versus the supplicant standing outside in the hall, the very fact that the same terminology of "royalty" *(malkût)* is also used in conjunction with him ("his royal throne") suggests a degree of equality between these two characters.

The terminology used for the "inner court" is significant (v. 1, and also previously in 4:11). This precise phrase *(ḥāṣar happĕnîmît)* is used elsewhere to refer only to the inner court of the temple in Jerusalem, first of Solomon's temple (1 Kgs 6:36; 7:12) and then of Ezekiel's imagined new temple (numerous instances throughout Ezek 40–44). As was the case with the descriptions about the palace's garden court (1:6-7), temple terminology is again used for the glories of state rather than the glories of religious worship (1:6-8). Language for the sacred (the holiness of YHWH) is transferred to the secular (the majesty of a human king).

When Ahasuerus sees Esther, he does not punish her but instead chooses to hold out his sceptre in invitation to an audience with him (v. 2). He sees in her the royal demeanor she displays, as her title is given, "Queen Esther." Ahasuerus addresses her as the queen, verbally acknowledging her status, when he speaks in the following verse (v. 3). (By verse 5, when the tension has diminished and he is anticipating a less formal and more genial occasion, he also relaxes his speech and refers to her without title, as "Esther.") He moves, to extend the sceptre—then she moves in response, to touch it.

The king follows the same progression as he did when initially becoming acquainted with Esther (2:15, 17). First he sees her, and then she gains his approval (v. 2). The language is the same as that used previously; just as Esther initially "won the favor" of Hegai and Ahasuerus (2:9, 17), so she now again "[wins] his favor." Esther does not need to say anything to gain this favor. Recalling that Ahasuerus has ignored her for thirty-three days, it seems that his attitude toward her had been "out of sight, out of mind." But then when he does see her, he melts. One might wonder what makes him approve her presence. Does he remember that he loves her (cf. 2:17)? Is he seeing again all those qualities that made him choose her for queen in the first place? Is he swayed, possibly even a bit frightened, by her newly found royal power? Is he impressed that she is courageous enough to dare to approach him?

When Ahasuerus does finally speak, his promise is as grandiose as his parties and year-long beauty treatments, promising "even to the half of my kingdom" (v. 3). He assumes that Esther wants something other than his company. Is this always the case when people approach him on the throne? Certainly it is the case when his male second-in-command comes to him (3:8-11; 6:4-11). When Ahasuerus first asks "What is it for you, Queen Esther?" (author's translation) and then refers to a physical item (half his kingdom), he reveals that he expects her to ask for some *thing*, a physical object. He does not reply, for instance, "Whatever you want me to do, I will do it." One should recall that this is a material king; he is aware of costly objects and the impressions they make (1:1-8) and is himself swayed by large gifts of money (3:9, 11). Esther surprises him when she responds not by asking for an expensive gift, but by asking that he *do* something. It is noteworthy that Ahasuerus replies in the passive voice, "it shall be given you," and that this passive recurs again in his promises in verse 6 and 7:2. He states that Esther shall have what she wants but does not obligate himself to provide it. This attitude is consonant with the character of the king as it has already been revealed. He does not decide and act for himself but instead has others do things for him; one sees that this is the case even when giving gifts to his wife.

Esther replies to his question by inviting him to a drinking party (v. 4). The inclusion of Haman could be troubling to Ahasuerus. If he expects that Esther still wants something from him (it is clear that he thinks the purpose of the party is for Esther to reveal her request, not that attendance at the party *is* her request; cf. v. 6), would he not think that also inviting Haman is odd? But not being too thoughtful a king, he does not question Esther's desire for Haman's presence and enthusiastically calls for him. By including Haman, Esther sets a trap for him; but because he becomes so proud after this party (5:12), he does not even see his demise coming.

Esther carefully crafts her response, presenting her proposal in ways that help her case. Her language is ingratiating. By repeating "the king" thrice in her statement (the final time in the Hebrew reads "to him"), she reminds this vain king of his own importance. She uses the rhetoric of pleasing: "If it please the king...." This is the language of the court, and Esther reveals herself to be an accomplished courtier, just as Memucan and Haman did earlier (1:19, 21; 2:4; 3:9). Esther also presents the drinking party as something that is done for him, "that I have prepared for the king" (v. 4). She knows that this lazy king does not like to do work but to have others prepare things (decisions, edicts, and so on) for him. The crowning touch is to suggest a drinking party, for this king will never say no to a party! In sum, Esther is assured that Ahasuerus will accept her invitation.

Ahasuerus's demand for Haman to come "quickly" highlights

his impulsiveness and his eagerness to get to the wine (v. 5). It is ironic that Ahasuerus will come at Esther's bidding, in contrast to Vashti's refusal to come at his bidding. That verse 6 refers to this occasion as "a drinking party of wine" (author's translation) reveals that it is a liquid party; the focus, as with previous palace parties, is on the alcohol served. It is not clear whether Esther is part of this cocktail party as one of the guests, or whether she serves the two men. At this point one hears echoes of the previous time when Ahasuerus and Haman were drinking together (3:15). It reminds the reader that, although all seems calm inside the palace, the city continues in its dismay and the danger of the situation still persists.

At the party the king follows the same sequence he did previously (v. 3): he raises a question about what Esther might want, but before waiting for an answer, he assuredly promises that whatever it is, she will have it (v. 6). Ahasuerus is even more emphatic now that Esther will have anything she desires, for he states so twice ("It shall be granted you, ... it shall be fulfilled"). And again he pledges her "even to the half of [the] kingdom." Esther responds in verses 7-8. Her statement in verse 7, "My petition and my request" (author's translation), serves to introduce what she says next in verse 8. Again, Esther carefully crafts her response. She parrots back to Ahasuerus the very words he uses in his speech to her (v. 6), subtly demonstrating that she "speaks his language." Esther replies with the same noun and verb combinations and in the same order: "grant a petition" and "fulfill a request." She, however, opts for active forms of the verbs, indirectly reminding Ahasuerus that he himself will need to act and take responsibility upon himself. (At the next party, he is indeed more active and decisive than is typical, so Esther's words seem to have had an effect upon him [7:8-9].) She also begins her response with two conditional statements that she knows to be the case: "If I have won the king's favor, and if it please the king." In verse 2 it is clear that she has indeed won his favor, and Ahasuerus's pleasure is evident throughout this episode in his zealous willingness to give her whatever she wants. Because he would say yes to these conditional statements, he automatically obligates himself to do what she asks next, to come to another drinking party. At the end Esther clinches a positive answer by vowing obedience. She knows that this king likes obedient queens—or at least he has made it quite clear that he dislikes disobedient queens. Her obedience, however, is partially feigned. At the next party, she does make her request; however, it is not for the bauble he seems to expect, but for clemency for her people.

Throughout this scene it is clear that Esther is acting strategically; she is playing her cards wisely. Even though she follows Mordecai's general advice to entreat Ahasuerus, she decides exactly *how* she will do it. Esther is savvy. Knowing how Mordecai's strategies are similar to those of Vashti gives the reader the sense that Mordecai, if he had advised Esther as to how she should proceed, would not be any more successful than Vashti was in dealing with the king. Esther, in contrast, pays attention to palace protocol, learning the likes and dislikes of the king. Closely observant during her years in the palace environment, she now uses all that knowledge and experience for her benefit.

The reader may wonder why Esther does not tell Ahasuerus what she wants the first time he asks. He is in a beneficent mood and would most likely have been receptive to what she would say. Why does she make him wait an additional day and attend a second party? This is much to ask of a king whose behavior tends toward the impulsive rather than the patient. Various possibilities for prolonging the request are that:

- she wants to get Ahasuerus even more drunk than he would be after the first party;
- she wants Ahasuerus to get accustomed to being with her again, after a month-long absence;
- she wants to heighten Ahasuerus's curiosity;
- she uses the additional time to build up the courage she will need;
- she plays a traditional female role (hostess) to assure Ahasuerus that she is not a threat to the male hierarchy;
- as he repeats his rash promises to give her whatever she wants, she wants Ahasuerus to feel an even greater commitment to fulfilling those promises;

- she wants Haman to feel safe and unthreatened, in order more fully to surprise him;
- she wants to please Ahasuerus, for if one party is good, two parties can only be better.

As the narrative does not provide an explanation, it is impossible to determine exactly what motive constitutes Esther's reason for delay. Whatever the explanation, this delay has the effect of keeping both the king and the reader in suspense. The fact that what she does ends up succeeding splendidly and that the rhetoric of her replies is so artfully composed suggests that waiting to request clemency for the Jews is a clever part of Esther's overall strategy.

Theological and Ethical Analysis

The question of power and how it is exercised comes to the fore in the events of this episode. For the first time in the story, power is used wisely and for a worthy purpose (Crawford 1999, 909). Differing types of power are represented by the characters. One might speak of authority, that is, one's position in society, where one exists within external hierarchical relationships. Ahasuerus, as the king, reflects this sort of positional power, as does Haman to a lesser extent. Esther, in contrast, acts instead from a sense of personal power rather than authority of position. Personal power can be seen not in terms of domination or force, but through actions to affirm oneself without harming others. In essence, power is a relational construct rather than an absolute quality. Esther's actions ideally reflect this aspect of power, as she effects change by means of relationality. Throughout this and the subsequent episodes, lines of power shift as relationships among the protagonists shift.

During these events, the characters reveal some of their finer moral qualities. Esther's courage and fortitude are especially admirable. As the scene opens, the reference to the third day reminds the reader, in shorthand fashion, that Esther has not eaten or drunk during that time; that Esther is able to carry her dangerous task through when weak from hunger and thirst demonstrates her physical as well as emotional strength. She likewise maneuvers through a difficult place in terms of her ethnic position—identification with the Persian royal hierarchy but solidarity with the Jewish people. Even Ahasuerus shows an admirable side in the episode. To this point in the story, the king has not appeared too attractive a figure, more a drunken, impulsive, lazy fool than a character worthy of admiration. But here Ahasuerus's generosity more strongly emerges as he willingly gives whatever might be asked. One is reminded of other glimpses of such generosity of spirit and of purse earlier, toward all the inhabitants of Susa (1:5, 7-8) and to all the inhabitants of the entire kingdom (2:18). Therefore, despite all his faults, Ahasuerus possesses an altruistic side as well.

Esther distinguishes herself from her predecessor Vashti and Vashti's method of doing things, displaying a different type of female leadership. The variances in the ways the two queens choose to act reminds the reader that there is never one "right" way to exert influence. Leadership styles can legitimately vary according to individual personality and talents. It appears that Esther has seen the first queen's style of conducting herself in a pressured situation and determined that that way would not be appropriate for her. Acting instead according to her own wisdom and intuition, she is successful in accomplishing what she desires. Vashti would not come into Ahasuerus's presence when desired, but Esther comes into his presence when *not* desired. She chooses to speak directly to his face, and she is full of words, full of ingratiating language—not Vashti's simple "No" for Esther. Moreover, Esther opts to voice her resistance to royal desires not in the public realm, as did Vashti (and also as did Mordecai), but in the private realm. In this ancient culture with its great importance on honor, she will not shame the king or his second-hand man with public dishonor.

Despite Esther's success, feminist readers may not be entirely comfortable with her method. Esther caters to the male whim, playing up to the male ego and pledging to comply with what a man wants her to do. The unquestionable phallic dimension of the scene, Esther's going forth to touch the male rod, only adds to the discomfort. To get what she wants, she plays the game on men's terms; one might argue that a true enactment of female power would be to make men play according to *women's*, or at least gender-free, rules. There are, therefore, real dangers in viewing Esther as a prototype of how the "ideal Jewish woman" ought to behave (Gendler 1976; see also

Fuchs 1982). In this sense Vashti's *modus operandi* is more attractive to modern feminist thought, for she does not appear to give away her queenly power. Though it is tempting to judge Esther's decisions and actions according to more modern feminist ideals, the reader must recognize that Persian society is not the gender-egalitarian environment one might desire. Perhaps Esther's approach, though conventionally female, is the pragmatic, even wise, choice; she does not attempt to change the system but works within it to achieve what she desires. The figure of Esther represents the fact that women in every generation have often had to wheedle and cajole to get what they need. One might note echoes of Jael, who likewise engages in conventional female activities (providing food and clothing); it is her action of playing into male expectations about female hospitality that enables her to defeat the enemy (Judg 4:17-22). Esther represents a strong and intelligent woman working within compromised circumstances. Regrettably, this situation is not too far removed from our own, centuries later. With regard to gender equity, current circumstances are also compromised, as modern readers note how, in the United States, few women and minority persons are permitted to the upper echelons of corporate executive ranks, and how women earn roughly 70 percent of male wages, a rate that has remained virtually unchanged for decades. Such patriarchal circumstances are certainly not what many women would want—nor, one might hazard a guess, what Esther would want. But at an intermediate stage before true gender equity is attained, perhaps Esther's approach to her problem represents a prudent, if not fully satisfactory, course of action.

CONVERSATIONS WITH HAMAN (5:9–6:14)

This episode follows Haman's actions, beginning immediately after he leaves Esther's drinking party and continuing during the rest of the day and throughout the night. He participates in three conversations during this time, two with his wife and friends and one with King Ahasuerus. Suspense mounts as Haman's situation becomes increasingly bleak. By the conclusion of the episode, one is left with another urgent question: will Haman really be successful in hanging Mordecai?

Literary Analysis

The action occurs at two venues: Haman's home and Ahasuerus's bedchamber. At his residence, Haman initiates a conversation with his wife and friends about his situation (5:9-14). The scene then shifts to the second venue as the narrative reports Ahasuerus's insomnia, recognition of an administrative omission, and correction of the problem (6:1-11). Then the scene shifts back again to the first setting, Haman's house, and another conversation with the same colleagues (6:12-14). In this way the episode is structured as an inclusio, with Ahasuerus's scene sandwiched between those at Haman's residence. Another of the story's reversals occurs during the events, when Mordecai wears finery and Haman wears mourning clothing.

The last scene (6:12b-14) mirrors the first (5:9-14). Many of the same elements are repeated, and the two function as parallel entities. As noted, both occur at Haman's residence, whither he arrives after spending time at the palace (5:9-10; 6:12a). He tells the same cast of characters—his wife Zeresh and his friends—about what has just happened to him (5:11-13; 6:13a). These listeners respond and speak with recognized wisdom (5:14; 6:13b). The events conclude with Haman on his way back to the palace (presumed [cf. 6:4]; 6:14).

The focus is primarily upon the protagonist Haman, and also upon Ahasuerus to a lesser degree. Mordecai does appear in the episode but is merely an object of the others' action. The purpose of the episode is not to further the plot line of the Jews' salvation, but to reveal more of Haman's character and to highlight his relationship with Mordecai. In literary terms, the focus is not upon plot but upon characterization. Haman's emotional life comes to the fore. The narrative reveals significantly more about his inner thoughts than about those of any other character, as it reports when he is joyful, angry, proud, pleased, and mournful. The book's sole instance of interior monologue, which is not very common in the Hebrew Bible, is used here for Haman (6:6). Even at pivotal moments when one might expect Mordecai's emotions to be reported, the narrative is silent about Mordecai and quickly returns attention to Haman's thoughts (6:12).

At this point the pace of the story escalates significantly. The episodes throughout the first parts of the book (chapters 1–4) progress leisurely, with several months or years elapsing between episodes. Now, however, events occur rapidly through to the end of the book. This episode begins immediately after the previous one, with Haman on his journey home after Esther's party, and it ends less than a day later, as he returns to the palace for her second party. In addition, there is a great amount of hurrying throughout the episode. Haman hurries to erect gallows; he goes immediately to Ahasuerus, who insists that he immediately carry out his wishes about Mordecai; then he hurries home for a brief visit until he is hustled away again.

Exegetical Analysis

The first scene at Haman's house reports how he sees Mordecai, who still refuses to do obeisance to him, on his trip home (5:9-14). When Haman spies Mordecai, he is sitting at the king's gate, which typically describes his location and occupation (5:9; cf. 2:19, 21; 3:2-3; 4:2, 6; 6:10, 12). There is, however, a change in the present depiction. Elsewhere, the emphasis is on the *place*, where Mordecai is. Now the emphasis lies more on Mordecai's action of *sitting*; he is sitting down and not moving his body as Haman would like. Yet the desired action also differs: previously Mordecai was chastised for not bowing (3:2-5), but now he is chastised for not standing up (Haman "observed that he neither rose nor trembled before him"). It is not Mordecai's chosen actions, per se, that trouble Haman, but Mordecai's attitude and perhaps also his mere presence. Initially, Haman was bothered by Mordecai's lack of proper obedience, but by this point in the story his hatred has developed so that it is against Mordecai's very person. What Haman desires from others is no longer merely obedience to the king's law and obeisance to himself, but actual fear ("trembling"). It appears that earlier Haman would have been satisfied if Mordecai had physically indicated obedience by bowing, even if not mentally agreeing that Haman warranted such honoring. But his demands have stepped up a notch, in now expecting fear. Haman reveals himself to be an insecure leader, one who wants his subjects to follow because of fear and not respect. As before, he responds with anger but does not directly display that anger at the spot. Haman replays his strategy of consulting with others behind closed doors: just as he and Ahasuerus made a deal to write an edict for the Jews' destruction (3:6-11), so now he plots with Zeresh and his friends.

Haman's emotions lie right on the surface throughout this scene. First the narrative reports how exceedingly joyful he is ("happy and good of heart," 5:9; author's translation). As the term "good of heart" *(ṭôb lēb)* is the same as that by which the tipsy Ahasuerus was described (1:10), it is likely that Haman is not fully sober after drinking Esther's wine (5:6). The reader is at first not sure why he is so happy after the party. Was the company engaging? Was entertaining music performed? Was there plentiful wine of excellent vintage? The reason is not revealed until 5:12: Haman is gladdened because he interprets an invitation to the queen's party as a great honor. Then, upon seeing Mordecai, he immediately becomes "infuriated," but just as quickly after being offered a solution he reverts back to his "good spirits" (5:14). The entire sequence reflects the earlier insubordinations of Vashti and Mordecai: happiness > dishonor > distress > solution > happiness (1:10–2:4; 3:1-15) (Beal 1999, 73). The same Hebrew adjective *śāmēaḥ*, "happy," neatly opens and closes this scene. Haman behaves in a mercurial fashion and, like Ahasuerus, tends to react from the gut and not think issues through rationally.

Haman, quite transparently, exhibits a great concern for honor. His interest lies not in the personal honor that comes from integrity, but instead in public honor and recognition from others. This characteristic is first seen in his two encounters with Mordecai, both in this episode and earlier (3:1-5). He also attempts to gain honor by bragging to his friends, calling them to his house for the express purpose of witnessing his greatness (5:11). One doubts that these individuals would even be considered "friends" if they were not willing to tolerate such an event. He boasts about three things: his bank account ("the splendor of his riches"); his abundant offspring ("the number of his sons"); and his social status, including the company he keeps ("all the promotions with which the king had honored him, and how he had advanced him above the officials and the ministers of the king," and now the queen's invitation). With regard to his progeny, it is not their quality (that is, whether they are good sons) but only their quantity that matters. One might compare the introduction to the book of Job, which likewise stresses Job's great number of possessions by including the number of his offspring (Job 1:1-3). And it is, of course, a touch of humor that Haman thinks that he needs to tell his wife how many sons he has.

Haman also brags about how he, and only he, was invited to drink with the queen and king. He boasts how "also Queen Esther did not bring with the king to the party which she gave (anyone) except me" (author's translation). All of his listeners must endure this long sentence before, at the very last word, finally getting to Haman's point—that he, alone, was included. Regarding the upcoming party, he places himself in the subject position and the queen as subsidiary: "I am invited by her" (rather than, for instance, "she invited me"). The way Haman chooses to phrase both of these statements about the parties emphasizes himself. In any event, Esther must have done an excellent job of covering up her probable distaste for the man, so that he remains none the wiser about her ethnic identity (Moore 1971, 60). The reader might wonder whether she had any idea how Haman would react to being invited. The coincidence of Haman's meeting Mordecai on the way home means that, if Haman's plan had been successful, an ironic side effect of her decision to include Haman at her drinking party would have been the hanging of Mordecai. This is surely something Esther did not anticipate, but she also most likely has no idea how close she comes to losing her cousin.

Haman's list of possessions and achievements is broken by a reference to how Mordecai's presence prevents him from fully enjoying them (5:13). He notes how "all of this is not sufficient (*šāwâ*) for me" (author's translation). This statement is difficult to translate with precision, but it is clear that Haman is saying that this action of Mordecai is not appropriate to his stature and importance. His use of the term *šāwâ* ("to be appropriate, to be sufficient, to be like"), a relatively rare word in Hebrew, is a sign of his self-aggrandizement. The other two uses of this term in the book of Esther refer to something not being appropriate to *the king* (3:8; 7:4). Through the use of this language, Haman subtly places himself in the king's role. In what sense does Haman find Mordecai's action to be inappropriate or insufficient? One possibility is in terms of outer prestige; other people will look down on Haman because he, despite being in the king's good favor, is insulted by Mordecai. Another option is in terms of his inner emotions, that his anger at Mordecai overrides his happiness at drinking with the queen and king. Likewise, not only Haman's words but also the narrative itself subtly compares Haman to the king. The same formula is used for Haman's approval as for Ahasuerus's approval of earlier plans: "this advice pleased Ahasuerus / Haman," immediately followed by a statement that the matter is carried out (1:21; 2:4; 5:14).

Zeresh plays the role of supportive wife, willingly listening to her husband's gloating and showing concern that he be happy (5:14). Yet she is intelligent and resourceful in her own right. When Haman cannot think what to do, she, along with his colleagues, comes up with a satisfactory solution. (In the Hebrew syntax the emphasis is upon her speaking.) What she proposes is that Haman take care of "the Mordecai problem" early. Instead of waiting the many months for the edict about non-Jews attacking Jews to be enacted, Haman should get rid of his enemy immediately: erect a gallows and have Mordecai hanged or impaled upon it. (The language could suggest either option, though most probably does not indicate death by means of hanging, but public exposure after death; see Bush 1996, 373, 414.) The result is that he would be saved from further humiliation. This action would shame Mordecai not only because public hanging is a dishonorable manner of death (a death befitting criminals; 2:23), but also because he would be revealed to the Jewish community as the linchpin of the problem. They would know that their imminent death is all because of a personal disagreement. The height of the gallows—somewhere around twenty-two to twenty-six meters (seventy-three to eighty-six feet), depending upon what measure of a cubit is used in calculation—is another larger-than-life element of this story. So high that everyone in Susa would see it, Mordecai's humiliation on the gallows must be as public as was Haman's humiliation (3:2-6). Zeresh's suggestion that Haman go to the king to enact this idea gives the impression that it would be so simple a matter that Haman would not even need to present a reason for this murder; as the kingdom's second in command, he has that much power. Even if such is not the case, Haman would be able to convince Ahasuerus to do what he wants, as he did before so successfully (3:8-11). If the gallows were already prepared, Mordecai could be taken care of immediately.

The middle scene in this episode begins in the king's bedroom (6:1-11). Ahasuerus cannot sleep, and the official Persian governmental records are brought in with the hope that they would have a soporific effect and that he, in a child-like fashion, could be read to sleep. When the report of the traitors' assassination attempt and Mordecai and Esther's saving of the king's life is discovered, it is determined that Mordecai had not ever been honored for his part in bringing the affair to light (2:21-23). Fittingly, it is the annals, literally "the book of remembrances," that is needed to help Ahasuerus and his servants remember to reward Mordecai. After the reader's attention has been focused upon all the more recent and more menacing events of Haman's edict, Esther's entrance, and Haman's gallows, this development reminds one of Mordecai's initial act of loyalty. The introduction of the scene recalls a time before danger entered the story.

Ahasuerus wonders, presumably, about the sound of someone entering the outer court, and that individual turns out to be Haman (6:4). When the narrative reports the reason why Haman is there—he wants to raise to the king the issue about hanging Mordecai—one wonders at his great haste. He is so impatient for Mordecai to be out of his way that he does not wait until reasonable hours but instead goes to bother the king during the middle of the night. Does he expect that Ahasuerus would be awake and willing to discuss business? Would he really dare to wake the king to solve his own personal problem? This action recalls Esther's coming before the king in the previous episode. Both stand before Ahasuerus to make a request (5:1). Haman, however, gives no indication that he fears for his life. It appears that the highest male official is not subject to the same rule about coming to the king without being called as is the queen, a distinction that makes clear where official power and influence in the Persian government are lodged.

When Ahasuerus asks Haman for a suggestion about how to recognize "the man whom the king wishes to honor," the passivity of the king's personality again becomes evident (6:6). Instead of devising an appropriate reward by himself, he delegates the responsibility to underlings and follows their advice to the letter (6:10; cf. 1:21; 2:4; 3:11). Ahasuerus even speaks in a passive fashion, asking "What was done?" rather than "What did I do?" about rewarding the persons who saved his own life (6:3). When the honor is granted, it is not Ahasuerus who performs it but his representatives. Here, as elsewhere, the king depends upon others to carry out the actual work of running a kingdom.

Upon hearing Ahasuerus's question, Haman's mind immediately jumps to himself; he assumes that is it he who is to be honored (6:6). This is the second time in this episode that Haman's egotism is emphasized (also 5:11-12), and at both places he reveals this character trait through his speech. This technique of characterization is far more effective than an objective narrative statement would be (e.g., "Haman is egotistical"), for one actually sees and hears Haman in action and is able to deduce this information for oneself. It is easy to judge Haman harshly for jumping to this conclusion so quickly, for being so blatantly self-centered. But Haman does have warrant, at least to a degree. After all, Ahasuerus has recently promoted Haman to the highest rank, so he must think more highly of Haman than of anyone else (3:1). Then he agreed fully with Haman's plan, giving him carte blanche (3:10-11). Also the queen—at least in Haman's mind—has just honored him (5:12). Now he is being asked to the king's bedchambers at this late hour.

Haman reverts from interior monologue (6:6) to exterior monologue (6:7-9). He responds with a lengthy suggestion for Ahasuerus, describing the actions of clothing the individual with the king's garments and being publicly led about by a royal official on one of the king's horses. As Haman speaks out loud, he gives the impression of envisioning himself receiving all of the items—the royal robes, the royal horse, the parade, the loud proclamation. The horse's "royal crown" is the same expression used to describe the queens' crowns, both Vashti's and Esther's (1:11; 2:17), and is likely a fabric headband in a particular color or design reserved for royalty (Salvesen 1999). Whether the image of a crowned horse reflects actual ancient practice (cf. Moore 1971, 65; Fox 2001, 77) or is merely another comedic element is uncertain. For all intents and purposes, an individual honored in this way will give the impression of royalty: he will look like the king. Moreover, Haman does not reply in the same fawning language as do others in the court ("if it please the king . . ."), but as though he imagines that he is speaking to his equal (Berlin 2001a, 58). Therefore, in this scene Haman continues to show his aspiration to be like a king (cf. 5:14).

Haman repeats the word "honor" four times throughout this brief section. It is as if Haman is rolling the phrase "the man whom the king wishes to honor" around on his tongue, deriving great pleasure merely from hearing it (Fox 2001, 76). Haman's idea is uniquely his. If Ahasuerus were deciding how to celebrate someone, he would tend to throw a party, as he does for himself (1:4) and for Esther (2:18). That it is Haman who chooses the reward means that it will be something about honor and public admiration. Each man shows off in different ways, and this contrast reveals the central concerns of each character: Haman wants personal respect from others, and Ahasuerus wants to strut his possesions.

Haman's surprise arrives at verse 10: the one honored will not be him, but Mordecai. That Haman is asked to perform this action would be offensive to one as aware of social distinctions as he is. The type of person whom he envisions to carry out this display is "one of the king's most noble officials," yet Haman has been promoted *above* all these officials (3:1). Haman probably does not see himself as an ordinary "official" anymore, and being asked to do the task of such an official would be insulting. Rather than the honor Haman expects to fall upon his own head, he receives shame. Why Ahasuerus feels a need for haste is not made evident, especially after having forgotten about the affair for years. Perhaps he is feeling guilty for having neglected to acknowledge Mordecai and wants the matter rectified as quickly as possible. He also wants the reward to be thorough, warning Haman to "leave out nothing." Does he harbor a suspicion that Haman will not relish this assignment? So even though the reward is delayed, it will be generous. Haman's dismay is that, in the end, he hurries that night not for Mordecai's death, but for his elevation.

The parade represents a vast alteration of appearance for Mordecai. The last time he was seen, he was in sackcloth and ashes (4:1-4); now he is in regal attire. This event also represents a contrast in Mordecai's actions; whereas he did not change clothes at Esther's request, he now willingly does so for Ahasuerus. The "royal robes" anticipate his own "royal robes" that Mordecai will later wear (8:15). Now he is only borrowing that regality, but then it will be his outright. He is led through "the open square of the city" (6:9, 11), which is the place where Mordecai tends to spend his time (4:6). All of his friends and colleagues who are also there, those who know Mordecai, would be certain to see him in his finery and to hear the royal accolades. Furthermore, if this celebration takes place near the king's gate, where it most likely would occur, it is fitting that Mordecai finally receives his reward where the conspiracy was plotted and discovered (2:21).

This incident highlights the contrast between Haman and Mordecai. Mordecai receives an honor because he has performed a heroic and loyal action, but Haman feels honored because he is very wealthy and was invited to a royal drinking party (5:11-12). It is clear why Haman agrees to lead Mordecai around—the king commands it. But a question left unanswered is why Mordecai permits Haman, of all people, to do this for him; after all, Mordecai has disobeyed royal behests in the past (3:2). He would not permit his own foster daughter to dress him, but now he allows an enemy (who is both an ancient enemy of his people and a personal enemy) to do just that and much more. Perhaps Mordecai's anticipation of how carrying out this deed would goad Haman is reason enough for his acquiescence.

As is frequently observed, this scene is built upon coincidences. Ahasuerus cannot sleep on the very night that Haman determines to hang Mordecai; one day later and Mordecai would have been dead. The section read to Ahasuerus from the annals just happens to be about Mordecai. At the very moment when Ahasuerus needs assistance from a courtier, Haman is outside his door. Ahasuerus does not name the recipient of the anticipated honoring, so Haman is permitted to think that it is himself. Throughout this scene, Ahasuerus's mind is on one thing (honoring Mordecai) and Haman's mind is on another (killing Mordecai, then honoring himself). Not surprisingly, the king's desires win out.

In the final scene Mordecai's response, after all the hoopla, is to go back to ordinary life (6:12-14). He returns to the king's gate, his typical location (2:21; 3:2; 4:2; 6:10), seemingly not affected at all. Haman's response, however, is a different story, as he rushes home in lamentation. His hurrying opens (6:12) and closes (6:14) this brief scene. Whereas the reason for Haman's haste to go to Ahasuerus's chambers in the middle of the night is not explicitly stated by the narrative, his reason to hurry away from the palace is; Haman is ashamed and he wants to cease his role as an object of public humiliation as soon as possible. His covered head anticipates, in grisly fashion, his covered head before his hanging or impaling (7:8). Haman picks up the mourning that the Jewish community, now on the morning of the fourth day, has just completed (4:1-3, 16). Yet even this very action highlights his vanity: the Jews grieved because of imminent death (and at Haman's hands, no less), whereas he mourns because his ego has been bruised.

Though it is only a few hours later than his first conversation with his colleagues (5:11-12), the change in mood at Haman's residence is great. Zeresh and Haman's colleagues speak again; their message, though, differs dramatically. She speaks with the voice of a seer, and her vision proves accurate. One wonders what, exactly, she sees in the events that cause her to predict doom for her husband. It is not the fact of Mordecai's Jewishness, for she knows of it earlier (5:13). Perhaps the sight of Mordecai in such fine clothing has made Zeresh see how rosy his future looks and, by extension, how bleak Haman's future must therefore be. Or perhaps, like Vashti, Zeresh is simply no longer willing to play the role of the "good wife," deferring to the pleasure of a difficult husband.

The act of falling is linked with Haman throughout this story, and the Hebrew verb *nāpal,* "to fall," links all his descents. First he causes the lot to fall, to determine a date for the Jews' destruction (3:7; 9:24). Then in this episode Ahasuerus speaks of falling in terms of Haman's tasks for Mordecai, commanding, literally, "Do not let a thing fall from everything you have said" (6:10). Both of these occurrences prefigure Haman's fall from grace; no longer will he cause things to fall, but he himself will be the object who ultimately falls. Zeresh and Haman's colleagues emphasize his falling through a three-fold repetition (evident only twice in translation) of *nāpal,* "to fall," in 6:13: "your downfall has begun, . . . [you] will surely fall." Later Haman falls upon Esther ("Haman fell upon the couch," 7:8; author's translation). And at his end, one can visualize him falling from the rope on which he is hanged (7:10). The concept of fate also links these occurrences. Haman wishes for the lot to fall, for it to predict the future for him. Now Zeresh and the others appeal to fate in predicting Haman's downfall.

Though appearing briefly and only in this episode, Zeresh is a strong presence in the story. The conflict is between two men, but it is two women (now Zeresh, then Esther) who determine the action (Levenson 1997, 92). Like Vashti, Zeresh is given little to say and do but has great influence, and also like Vashti, she flouts Persian law. There is a royal decree on the books that all men are to be masters in their own households, arising from a warning about wives giving honor to their husbands and not speaking against them (1:16-22). Just as was Memucan's concern, Zeresh is a noble lady and Haman an official of the king (1:18). In Haman's household, however, it appears more the case that Zeresh rules; she tells him what he should do, and he does it (5:14). Also, when predicting his demise in such stark fashion, Zeresh certainly "speaks against" her husband. Zeresh's blatant violation of this royal edict draws into question its general efficacy and makes the reader wonder how many other households in the kingdom are still ruled by women, despite Memucan's edict of several years ago.

Servants play unobtrusive but vital roles throughout the episode. With regard to Zeresh's proposal for Mordecai's disposal, 5:14 reads, literally, "Let them make a gallows ... and let them hang Mordecai upon it." Presumably servants are the individuals intended to do the dirty deed, but they are not even identified as such. One would think that the carpenters erecting this high gallows would wonder *why* they are given such a job, especially with such a tight deadline of overnight completion, and for *whom* the gallows is needed. Speculation and rumor would be on the rise among the ranks of the servant community. In the royal bedroom the servants are likewise effaced by the narrative. The "king's servants" in 6:5 are presumably the same individuals who bring the annals and discover Mordecai's story (6:1-2) and then lead the horse (6:9), but such is not clearly stated. In quite a contrast with all the names at 1:10, servants are represented in both scenes by the same impersonal "they" seen also at 4:12 and 7:10. At the episode's conclusion, it is royal servants (here the king's eunuchs) who whisk Haman away (6:14). The eunuchs are involved in what seems to be their typical role throughout the story, conveying persons and things to and from royal places, as they do (or at least attempt to do) with Vashti (1:10-12), Persian young women (2:3), Esther (2:8, 16), and information (4:4, 8, 9, 10, 12).

Theological and Ethical Analysis

Character flaws in prominent and powerful individuals have the potential to cause great harm. Leaders can govern only as well as the ethical strength their personalities allow. How often throughout world history has seen corruption at the top led to great suffering for the common folk. In the Esther story, nowhere else are a leader's vices drawn so clearly. The reader sees how Haman's character is built upon greed and pride. Haman's avarice is the type that can never be satisfied; he wants all to recognize him, and he will go to all ends to satisfy his drive for revenge. He represents the kind of people who are most dangerous, who hold on to their anger and plot retaliation. It is easier to deal with the types like Ahasuerus, who get angry, act immediately upon that anger, and then let their annoyance pass out of their systems. Concern for personal honor also runs throughout the episode, both in Haman's relentless desire to be venerated and in Mordecai's receiving public honor. Mordecai's loyalty is emphasized, as his faithful action to the crown is finally given its just reward. He is made into a public example, a role model, for all the residents of Susa.

Haman's character is a prime example of how societal racism and prejudices are bred by the personal insecurities of their instigators. Unable or unwilling to acknowledge their own personal moral failings, such persons project their feeling of inadequacy upon others. It is how intolerance is born. Haman's numerous insecurities lie on the surface of his personality. In this figure the narrative presents a quintessential example of the figure of the fool from the biblical wisdom tradition. He is arrogant (Prov 16:5), proud (Prov 29:23), boastful (Prov 27:1-2), vents his anger (Prov 29:11), and speaks in haste (Prov 29:20). He has been richly blessed; his life should be ideal, with a good job, a supportive spouse, children who make him proud, and plenty of money. Yet his petty worries about revenge keep him from recognizing all that has been bestowed upon him. Haman's own dissatisfaction with his current circumstances leads him to act outwardly against others, to use them to fill what he feels to be lacking in his own life.

A theological concept running throughout the biblical tradition is that of Zion theology, YHWH's inviolable covenant with David and Jerusalem. The promise is that David's people (the Israelites) and place (Zion) will endure forever, that enemies will not be successful against them (e.g., 2 Sam 7:8-16; Ps 89:3-4, 19-37). Therefore, a quality of Jewish chosenness is strongly represented in the Hebrew Bible, especially in the divine promises to David and his descendents. A component of this theological premise is that even other peoples, the Gentiles, will recognize the Jews' chosenness and invincibility—just as Zeresh recognizes (e.g., Isa 2:1-4; 45:14-23; 60:1-18). It is the Jews' Jewishness that prompts Zeresh's foretelling. Such assurance of Jewish existence is the same principle earlier suggested by Mordecai (4:14), an "absolute principle, independent ... even of the moral condition of Jewry" (Fox 2001, 250). In struggles, the Jews have some unique quality that renders victory certain. Zeresh reflects other Gentiles in biblical literature who predict Jewish success, for instance, Nebuchadnezzar (Dan 3:28-30) and Achior (Jdt 5:5-21). Unlike these individuals, however, Zeresh provides no reason for her claim; to her assertion about Haman's fall before the Jews, she adds no explanation, such as "the Jews will prevail because their god YHWH is with them," nor does she refer to any of the biblical statements that predict Israelite victory over Amalek in the promised land (cf. Exod 17:14-16; Deut 25:17-19; Num 24:20). In the larger biblical tradition, the Israelites, or Jews, are special because it is God who has chosen them and God who will sustain them forever. In this story, however, the Jews' inviolability is at the human, not the divine, level: they will prevail because of some aspect intrinsic to their Jewishness and not because of divine assistance.

How often one hears the expression "some people have all the luck" about someone whose circumstances appear rosy. When speaking in theological terms, however, it is tempting to see only a fine line between luck and blessing. Are fortuitous circumstances and unexpected turns of events, sheer coincidence or a reward for an upstanding moral character? In one sense, then, one is led to question whether luck should be viewed in terms of an ethical category. In the Esther story, luck is clearly on Mordecai's side, in that he is honored for his loyalty rather than punished for his disloyalty (as Vashti was, and as Haman will be for his misperceived disloyalty of violating the queen). Luck, however, is clearly against Haman. The concept of fate is introduced again in this episode, by the coincidental activities during the king's sleepless night and by Zeresh and the friends' prediction of the Jews' success. This scene reflects the role of chance in human events. The book of Qoheleth similarly suggests that people are not in control of their own destinies, but that "time and chance happen to them all, for no one can anticipate the time of disaster" (Qoh 9:11-12). Despite his attempts to manipulate time (3:7), Haman does not anticipate his own coming disaster. Human beings frequently appear to be dependent upon the whim of chance, which determines whether we ride the royal steed—or lead it—down the path of life. The numerous coincidences throughout the episode tempt some interpreters to see an invisible divine hand, a divine providence, arranging events in such an improbable sequence (Bush 1996, 418; Moore 1971, 67; Crawford 1999, 915; Clines 1984b, 307). Yet again the text is ambiguous, attributing nothing to the deity. In this episode, the overall perspective still remains that of fate, not of theology.

ESTHER'S REVELATION (7:1–8:2)

This episode relates the events of Esther's second drinking party. King Ahasuerus again inquires about Esther's desires. This time, however, she reveals Haman as the perpetrator of her people's destruction. He is hanged in punishment, and Esther and Mordecai receive his property.

Literary Analysis

The episode begins immediately upon the conclusion of the last episode, and there is not a strong division between them. Because 7:1 repeats the detail of 6:14, Haman's travelling to Esther's party, it serves as a logical place of division. Actions occur quickly, so quickly that Haman is not even permitted to complete what will be his final discussion with his wife and friends, but is whisked away mid-conversation (6:14). The events continue at breakneck speed, with hardly a moment to think, and this fact is especially pertinent when one realizes that by the conclusion of this brief scene, everything is topsy-turvy from the situation at its beginning. No longer the underdogs, Esther and Mordecai have some security, and the one who decreed their deaths is now himself dead and gone. Another reversal is evident: the very gallows that Haman built for Mordecai is used instead to hang him, and the disgrace he planned for Mordecai is now his.

As the reader began the scene of Esther's first party (5:1-8), it was with the question, *Will Esther be killed?* now, however, the overriding curiosity is, *What will Esther ask?* This episode begins as a direct parallel to Esther's previous party. Ahasuerus and Haman come quickly, there is much drinking of wine, and Esther uses ingratiating language throughout. The terminology of 7:1-3*a*, in fact, is such a verbatim repetition of 5:5*b*-7*a* that the only way one knows that this is a new occurrence is through the descriptions "on the second day" and "again" (7:2). Only at 7:3*b* does the language diverge from the first instance. As Esther's answer begins to deviate from her earlier reply, the dramatic tension of the scene escalates. One can imagine her two party guests hanging on her every word.

The entire episode occurs in one setting: Esther's chambers, the room where she hosts her parties. Though Ahasuerus does travel outside it for a moment, the reader does not follow him there, as the narrative focus remains with Esther. Two notable instances of a shift in point of view occur. At 6:14, the reader stands at Haman's house with Zeresh and his friends, watching Haman being taken away. Immediately following, the point of view changes and the action is presented from inside the party chambers, and the reader watches Haman and Ahasuerus come in. A similar shift occurs at 7:7*b*-8*a*. First, the reader sees the scene through Haman's eyes: "for he saw that the king had determined to destroy him." But at the next statement, the reader observes the scene instead through Ahasuerus's eyes, as he reenters the room, seeing that "Haman had thrown himself on the couch where Esther was reclining."

The focus of this episode is upon three of the protagonists: Esther, Ahasuerus, and Haman. The king, for the first time in the story, becomes more active in making his own decisions. Esther is predominantly referred to by her title here, more consistently than she has been before, as "Queen Esther" and "the queen," rather than just "Esther." This detail of nomenclature makes her character appear more regal, powerful, and authoritative. Furthermore, Esther demonstrates how she has grown into a mature thinker, able to speak eloquently and anticipate others' responses. Haman and Ahasuerus, as before, continue to be presented as emotional; the narrative tells us the fear and anger, respectively, that they are feeling. Even Esther, though no descriptive statement identifies her inner state, comes across as more emotionally engaged than she has to this point, even when anticipating her own death (4:16). Her passion comes through as she speaks.

Exegetical Analysis

As Ahasuerus and Haman begin the party with Esther, the focus again is on drink. They go in specifically "to drink" ("to feast" in the NRSV; 7:1), and the narrative notes how all occurs "as they were drinking wine" (7:2). Reference to alcoholic drink continues throughout the episode, in 7:7 as "the drinking party of wine" and in 7:8 as "to the house of the drinking party of wine" (author's translations). As was Esther's first party, this is also a cocktail party. Esther appears to be trying to make Ahasuerus, and Haman as well, feel comfortable, to give him what she knows he enjoys so that he will relax and be in a receptive mood for her revelation. The irony is that, as the decision for the Jews' destruction was sealed with drink (3:14), so the decision for Haman's destruction comes in the midst of drink.

The reference to this action as occurring on the second day highlights the fact that this conversation has all happened before (7:2). That Ahasuerus again inquires as to Esther's request makes clear that he does not think that this party *is* her request; she wants more than his company. The language about petition and request, promising her up to half the kingdom, is exactly the same as he used earlier (5:3, 6). Even with a day to think over his response, the king is still ready to give Esther anything.

Esther's use of rhetoric in 7:3-4 is flawless. She knows how easily Ahasuerus can be manipulated, and she does so through the manner by which she presents her argument. As before, Esther begins by alluding to the fact that she has won Ahasuerus's favor and that he delights in her (cf. 5:8). She again uses deferential terminology, referring to him as "king," but this time she personalizes her reply: "If I have won *your* favor, O king" (emphasis mine). The combination of these two details serves to remind Ahasuerus that he is in charge, that he is king and accountable for what happens in his kingdom. Esther knows that because his answer to both of the first questions is yes, that she indeed does please him, it will make him feel obligated to say yes to what she asks. Esther must, by this time, recognize that all suggestions made to the king tend to meet with his approval (1:21; 2:4; 3:11; 6:10). By her very choice of courtier language she reminds him that his tendency is to approve others' requests and suggestions, so that he will do the same for hers when she presents it.

Whereas the conversation about her desire at the first party moved rather slowly, with each participant making lengthy statements, now Esther appears eager to make her petition. Echoing Ahasuerus's petition and request phraseology back to him, she also matches his statement with the same verb he uses, "to give" *(nātan),* in the passive. Esther asks for life, life for herself and for her people (7:3). Ahasuerus's initial reaction would be to wonder what in the world she is talking about. As he most likely expects her to request an object of some sort, Esther's statement would surprise him considerably. Then she continues to explain what she means (7:4). It is probably more effective that Esther presents her concern in this fashion, rather than giving the explanation first. She first gets Ahasuerus's attention, causes him to sit up, brings him out of an inebriated stupor, and sobers up his mind so that he will be able to comprehend what she says next and will have a clear enough head to be capable of responding properly.

In her explanation, Esther is careful to present the situation in as nonthreatening a fashion as possible. She is counting on Ahasuerus having forgotten his involvement, just as he forgot to reward Mordecai (6:3). Esther states the problem in the passive voice, with an indefinite subject: "We have been sold." If Esther were to reveal, initially, the person who did the selling, if she were to present the events as they actually occurred, it would make both men feel threatened and defensive. Instead, keeping her language impersonal recruits Ahasuerus's sympathies and makes him curious as to who would have done such a thing. It also makes Haman feel safe, thinking that perhaps Esther will not reveal his guilt or that perhaps she does not even know that he was behind the decree. Esther, however, puts herself in an extremely vulnerable position. She "unmask[s] the villain, but she also . . . unmask[s] herself" (Moore 1971, 74).

Esther makes it clear that she feels solidarity with the Jewish people. She twice refers to herself and them in parallel phrases: "my life . . . and the lives of my people" and "I and my people." Using the description "my people" rather than "the Jews" plays upon Ahasuerus's affection and approval of her. If he saves *her* life, she implies, he will also have to save *their* lives. She and they are a package; anything done for her is contingent upon the same being done for them. Quoting from the edict itself (3:13), Esther also stresses the violence planned for this population, repeating all of the three separate verbs to refer to the killing ("to be destroyed, to be killed, and to be annihilated"). The quotation draws in full relief her identification with the fate of this doomed population.

The final statement of 7:4 is difficult in the Hebrew. It could be translated, as the NRSV does, as "but no enemy can compensate for this damage to the king." Another option is "for there is no distress comparable with damage of the king." (For fuller discussions, consult Paton 1908, 260-62; Fox 2001, 282; Bush 1996, 427-28.) The basic gist is understandable. Esther is presented with a dilemma about loyalties: loyalty to her people versus loyalty to the crown. She weighs the trouble caused to her people with the damage that would be caused to Ahasuerus if he were told about the situation (perhaps causing him shame, or grief, or money; for the last, see Fox 2001, 84-85). She feels—or at least presents her feelings in this way—a divided loyalty, for the pain of the Jews and for the welfare of the king. That the Jews are to be killed, and not just sold as servants, is what causes her to decide that she must tell Ahasuerus. Putting herself in the "we" of the hypothetical slaves, or servants, would have been a stretch for the king to hear, to compare the queen of Persia to one of such a low social position as a slave. Esther, in this statement, also insinuates that the one who so acted is an enemy to the throne and not solely an enemy of her people. That this one is later revealed as the highest official in the kingdom represents a huge scandal.

Would it really have been permissible to Esther for the Jews to be enslaved or indentured? Probably not. In her response, she appears rather melodramatic, and this phrase can be seen as part of her manner of overstatement. Esther is making a point, to say that she can be flexible and patient up to a certain level, but that the situation has now surpassed that level. She presents herself as a tolerant person, willing to put up with a certain amount of abuse for her people for the sake of the kingdom's good; it is murder to which she objects. This is what, she avers, causes her to speak out.

Ahasuerus can stand the suspense no longer and demands to know the identity of the perpetrator of Esther's agony (7:5). Esther has played up Ahasuerus's emotions, getting him angry before revealing who deserves to be the object of that anger. The reader may wonder whether Ahasuerus is sincere that he does not suspect what Esther is talking about or whether he may be feigning ignorance. Has he so thoroughly forgotten his agreement to a death warrant for an entire segment of the population that even Esther's mention of it does not recall it to mind? Or *does* he remember, being worried whether Esther will reveal that he is implicated or blame only Haman as the instigator?

Ahasuerus's question is succinct and staccato, "Who is he, and where is he?" six short monosyllabic words in the Hebrew. The next phrase reads, literally, "who filled his heart to do this." This is the only place in the Hebrew Bible where the expression "to fill a heart" *(mālē' lēb)* occurs. The phrase appears to have an ethical sense, to fill the heart with negative desires. A similar expression is found in Exodus 15:9, "to fill a soul" *(mālē' nepeš)*. This expression implies a heart filled with evil intentions, in the context of an enemy (Pharaoh) intending destruction toward Israel, and it is likely that the phrase used in the book of Esther has a similar connotation. This comparable terminology is a subtle connection that links the Esther story with the story of the exodus; as Esther resembles Moses, now Haman resembles the Pharaoh who wishes harm to the Hebrews.

Esther matches Ahasuerus's question with a similarly brief and curt reply of her own: "A foe and enemy, this wicked Haman" (7:6). One can imagine Esther standing up, pointing her finger, and spurting out these words (Fox 2001, 86). Analogous to her tripartite description of Haman's action (7:4), Esther uses three synonyms to describe Haman himself: "foe," "enemy," and "wicked." The repetition emphasizes his character as thoroughly evil. Not only does Esther reveal Haman, but she must also stress his wickedness, so that she is able to switch the king's allegiance from Haman to herself quickly and decisively. Only now does it become clear to both Ahasuerus and the reader why Esther has invited Haman to her drinking parties: she wants to frame him.

With Haman right there, under their and all the servants' noses, it is impossible for him to escape. Until this revelation Haman does not know that Esther is connected to Mordecai. Therefore, even if he were seriously worried about Zeresh's prediction of his demise and expecting Mordecai to be on the lookout for him, Haman would not anticipate anything to happen at the queen's party; he would feel safe in this environment. Responding to Esther's revelation in surprise and terror, he displays the same fear before Esther that he wanted Mordecai to show him (5:9). Haman is the first non-Jew to be afraid of the Jews (represented by Esther), though many more will show fear before the story concludes (8:17; 9:2).

Ahasuerus is so furious that he is unable to remain in the same room with Haman (7:7). His anger is quickly ignited and burns hot. Getting up, he goes out into the garden without saying a word, nor does the narrative provide the reason. Is his motive rational (he wants to get some fresh air to help him think clearly after his sleepless night) or emotional (he wants to cool off his anger before responding)?

The reader also has no idea how Haman has been reacting through the queen and king's conversation. Not until 7:6 does the narrative turn its attention back to him. Haman interprets Ahasuerus's response as "evil from the king plotted against him" (author's translation). It represents a fine example of poetic justice, for as Haman himself is "evil" (Hebrew *rāʿâ*), now he is to receive "evil" *(raʿ)*. And as the Jews were in danger of being destroyed (7:4), now Haman is threatened with destruction. Yet how odd it is to think of Ahasuerus, this ruler who always goes to others for advice, as plotting anything at all. Perhaps Haman projects this aspect of his own personality upon the king. In response, Haman pleads to Esther; this proud, proud man now humbles himself. In his mind, if Esther made the charge against him, she can also take it back, and no harm will be done. His response is scandalous for two reasons: in prostrating himself, Haman performs the very action he punished Mordecai for not doing, and he begs from one of the very persons he had condemned. That Haman chooses to ask her and not Ahasuerus indicates that he believes Esther to have power in the court and influence over the king. The tables are turned. A moment ago, Esther was in the position of *making* a request; now she is in the position of being able to grant someone else's request. Just as she had asked for her "life" (*nepeš;* 7:3), he now asks her for his "life" *(nepeš)*.

Upon returning to the party, Ahasuerus spies Haman fallen on Esther's couch and suspects the worst. When he asks, "Will he even assault the queen in my presence, in my own house?" the reader understands what causes Ahasuerus's anger toward Haman. Ahasuerus does not refer to Esther as "my wife"; he is not speaking here as an indignant husband in defense of his wife's sexual honor. Instead, he addresses her as "the queen," showing that he interprets Haman's actions as an affront to the crown. Haman's attempt to kill, and now (from Ahasuerus's point of view) to seduce, Esther is not a personal violation, but a crime against the state. Though it might be argued that Ahasuerus's misperception is intentional and he feigns misunderstanding as an excuse to punish Haman, interpreting his response as a genuine misunderstanding of Haman's actions fits better with the king's characterization as more emotional than rational.

The narrative transition from 7:8 to 7:9 is abrupt; immediately after Ahasuerus speaks, Haman's face is covered. Such face covering before sentencing for hanging is unusual, though it may reflect a later Greco-Roman custom for condemned persons. Whatever the provenance, the covering of his head while mourning acts as a literary device to echo visually Haman's prior humiliation (6:12). Now Haman does have something to grieve—the loss of his life and not only his pride. The referent for the "they" who cover his face is not fully clear. The most likely option is the servants, the ones who bring Haman to the party (6:14) and are mentioned one verse later (7:9). This interpretation would suggest that the servants had been present in the room throughout all the proceedings, listening and ready to respond. Whoever they are who perform this deed do it very quickly and on their own, without a direct order from the king.

Harbona, one of the eunuchs, gives Ahasuerus the hint he needs, pointing out the gallows that Haman had had made for

Mordecai, "whose word saved the king" (7:9). Previously, Ahasuerus's advice has only come from his officials; now, however, a servant ascertains an appropriate response. The way that Harbona explains the situation further implicates Haman by reminding the assembled company of Mordecai's revelation of the assassins' plot—Mordecai is a good person, so by implication Haman must be a bad one. At this point it becomes clear that the gallows are at Haman's house, a detail not included earlier (5:14). The reader realizes that Haman not only wanted to hang Mordecai, but also wanted the deed performed in his own front yard so that he would be reminded of Mordecai's shame every time he left or returned home. Ahasuerus, in the most decisive statement he has made, commands the servants to hang Haman on that gallows. His hanging "on the gallows that he had prepared for Mordecai" is a perfect, albeit grisly, statement of poetic justice. In his death, Haman, the one so concerned about public honor, will be publicly shamed in front of his own home. Furthermore, because he built the stake so tall, everyone will know his humiliation.

Even though Haman receives the punishment one might argue he deserves, he is punished for a crime he did not commit. He did not attempt to kill the queen, as Esther suggests, for he did not know of Esther's Jewishness nor of her relation to his enemy Mordecai. Nor does he try to rape the queen, as Ahasuerus understands him to be doing.

Ahasuerus's anger in this episode is reminiscent of his anger toward Vashti at the beginning of the story (1:9–2:4). That the same Hebrew term for "anger" (ḥēmâ) is used in all places links them together in the reader's mind (1:12; 2:1; and here in 7:7, 10). This scene with Haman follows the same sequence as did Ahasuerus's anger at Vashti: Vashti and Haman do something Ahasuerus does not like, he becomes angry, a solution is suggested, Ahasuerus has the solution carried out, and finally he becomes calm again. His emotions come quickly but are just as quickly dissipated. Haman also behaves the same way with regard to Mordecai, becoming angry, finding a solution, and returning to a good mood (3:2-15; 5:9-14), copying the king's way of coping with a personally distressing situation. Ahasuerus's and Haman's choices of solutions are likewise strikingly similar. When faced with someone doing something they do not like, they find a way to get rid of the person: Ahasuerus banishes Vashti, Haman tries to kill Mordecai, and Ahasuerus now kills Haman. Then Ahasuerus simply replaces the vanished individual with another person, having Esther replace Vashti (2:17) and having Mordecai replace Haman (8:2)—and all returns to equilibrium.

In 8:1-2 Ahasuerus gives the house of Haman to Esther, which she gives over to Mordecai after he reveals to Ahasuerus his relationship to the queen. Clearly women are assumed to have the legal right to own property. Therefore, even though Esther does not ask for a physical object as her request, Ahasuerus nonetheless gives her one. Ahasuerus seems anxious to resolve things quickly, for as soon as Haman has been taken care of, he disposes of Haman's property, bequeathing all of this "on that day." Haman's "house" refers not just to the building itself, but to all of his possessions, that is, his household. Though one might expect that the estate would be inherited by Haman's sons or Zeresh, the text probably reflects a Persian practice that the property of criminals reverts to the crown. Ahasuerus already received ten thousand talents of silver from Haman's financial portfolio, for agreeing to a decree against the Jews, and now he will have the remainder of Haman's wealth as well. After Esther receives Haman's household, she establishes Mordecai over it, perhaps as an overseer or trustee of the property. When she was a child, he cared for her; now that she is in a position so to do, Esther cares for him. This transfer represents ultimate shame to Haman, for the description of Haman as "the enemy of the Jews" serves as a reminder of that rivalry. Haman's wealth, of which he is so proud, is not passed on through his family, but goes to someone who is an ancient foe.

Mordecai also receives a gift from the situation. Taking his signet ring back from (the dead body of?) Haman, Ahasuerus gives it to Mordecai. This ring represents administrative power (3:10-11). Ahasuerus gives to Esther wealth (Haman's household), but to Mordecai he gives political clout. Thus at the conclusion of this episode, Mordecai has taken Haman's place on two levels:

socioeconomically (represented by the house) and politically (represented by the signet ring). Mordecai now has the things of which Haman was most proud, his position and his possessions (5:11). Yet he is a beneficiary of all of this only because of Esther's own position and her generosity; it is she who tells Ahasuerus "what he was to her." In the previous episode, Mordecai received honor for what he, with Esther's assistance, had done. Now, however, he receives honor solely because of his relationship to Esther. Mordecai's success comes to him because he knows people in high places.

Theological and Ethical Analysis

At the close of the episode, the result is viscerally satisfying: revenge is accomplished, Haman receives his just deserts, hoisted on his own petard. What he attempted to do to others is done to him, a prime example of "what goes around, comes around." The loyalty of Mordecai, "whose word saved the king," is directly juxtaposed with "the wicked Haman." Like the hoods being removed from a Ku Klux Klan lynching mob, Haman's racism is now fully revealed for the world to see his true nature. Yet the result is not as morally unambiguous as it appears at first glance. Haman receives the death penalty without any trial or even a chance to explain himself. Though he asks for mercy, none is even considered for him. Esther merely asks that her life and that of the Jews be saved, but what she receives instead is the death of the enemy. Ahasuerus does not pause to examine his own complicity; he takes the easy solution, to kill (literally) the problem rather than try to resolve it. As persuasive with the king as she has proved to be, Esther could have kept Ahasuerus from giving Haman the death penalty, might have attempted to convince him to find some other sort of punishment for Haman. Though Haman is, in Moore's often repeated assessment, a "falling" and not a "fallen" foe (1971, 74), he could have been rendered similarly powerless by a demotion from his influential political office. The episode, therefore, raises many questions as it provides gratifying outcomes.

With regard to ethnic relationships, norm and "other"—Persian and Jewish—begin to emerge and converge in this episode.

Like any person with allegiance to more than one community, Esther is learning how to juggle loyalties to both parts of her identity without renouncing either aspect of her being. The art of such integration is not always easy. Esther comes out from a hidden existence as she chooses a new position of resistance. In addition to a victorious event, it is also a liberating moment. Lesbian and gay individuals, for instance, often speak of the freedom they feel when finally revealing a side of their being they have kept hidden. The episode shines light on the faceted nature of human existence. At initial encounter, people tend to know one another by limited and obvious characteristics (Mordecai the Jew, Esther the queen, Haman the official). Yet never is such a one-dimensional view ever accurate. When anyone "comes out," as these characters do, one sees her or his fuller connections with others (Esther's cousin Mordecai, Esther the Jew, Haman the enemy). One of the joys of human nature is the intricate web of relationships among people; after all, no man is an island. Haman's tactical error was to assume that the young woman summoned to the citadel would have connection only to the crown. There is a great disservice—to say nothing of potential mortal danger—in assuming that the first side we see of a person is the only one that is important.

The question of finance is indelibly linked with that of justice. In the Hebrew Bible, there is a strong prophetic tradition that draws a connection between justice and economics, maintaining that it is impossible to perform social and religious righteousness without also considering economic righteousness (e.g., Mic 3:9-12; Amos 2:6-8; 4:1-3; Isa 1:21-23). The financial aspects of the events lead the reader to consider their connection to the concern for justice also inherent to the scene. Esther uses the language of money when speaking to Ahasuerus of compensation and slavery, setting up a tension between freedom and money. She and Mordecai receive financial gain through Haman's inheritance, yet one wonders if financial benefit from the defeat of an enemy is significantly different from the plunder the Jews later refuse to take (9:10, 15). In making social policy decisions, however, issues of justice are never as pure and unclouded as one would like, for money is often a factor. The attempt to right certain injustices often leads to the formation of new injustices, an inherent tension. For example, with the eradication of Haman a social justice is achieved, and financial compensation for the victims is not unreasonable. Yet in rendering this reparation, a widow and orphans (Haman's family) are deprived of their livelihood. The relationship between social justice and economic justice, therefore, is sometimes ambiguous, and decisions are often not simple and clear-cut. In making such policy determinations should a society seek to maintain the greatest good for the greatest number of people? to attempt to redress old wrongs? to address the most immediate needs first? Yet when deciding any public policy, a just society must also keep in mind the poor who will inevitably fall through the cracks—the foreigners, the widows, the orphans (cf. Exod 22:21-24; Deut 24:17-22).

ESTHER PLEADS, MORDECAI WRITES (8:3-17)

This episode reports how Esther again approaches Ahasuerus to make a request of him. She asks that a new decree be written to revoke Haman's decree, and Ahasuerus gives her and Mordecai the authority to so write. Mordecai authors the new edict, which permits the Jews to defend themselves when attacked, it is distributed throughout the kingdom, and the population rejoices upon hearing it.

Literary Analysis

The focus of this episode is primarily upon the protagonists Esther and Mordecai, and only secondarily upon Ahasuerus. It divides fairly neatly in half, with the first events centering upon Esther (vv. 3-8), and the following events centering upon Mordecai (vv. 9-17). The relative timing of the events is not precisely delineated. The narrative does not specify how much time has passed since the previous events, whether Esther speaks to the king soon after receiving his gifts (8:1-2), or whether a period of time elapses, although haste is more likely considering the urgency of her task. Yet the writing of this new decree occurs over two months after the writing of Haman's decree (3:12), which necessitates either that Esther delays in speaking to Ahasuerus or that the royal scribes delay in writing the edict (v. 9).

The episode consists of repetitive elements. The present scene in which Esther approaches (vv. 3-6) resembles the earlier two scenes when she came before Ahasuerus (5:1-7; 7:1-10), and the description of Mordecai's decree (vv. 8-14) imitates closely that of Haman's earlier decree (3:10-15). This strong parallelism suggests reversals on various levels. That Mordecai's sackcloth (4:1-2, 4) is replaced by royal finery (v. 15) provides a strong *visual* image; that the Jews' cries of lamentation (4:3) are replaced by cries of rejoicing (vv. 15b-16) provides a strong *aural* image; and that their fasting (4:3, 16) is replaced by drinking and eating (v. 17) provides a strong *gustatory* image. Moreover, the Jews' feelings of worry and fear (4:3) are supplanted by the non-Jews' fear (v. 17). Because Mordecai and Haman have been presented as opposite figures and enemies, it is significant that not only does the new edict itself reverse the past edict, but also Mordecai's authorship reverses Haman's previous authorship.

Much of the suspense, carefully developed to this point, is released during this episode. The new edict enforcing the Jews' retaliation is given. Even though it has not yet been enacted—that is, the thirteenth of Adar has not yet arrived—the reader takes a cue from the Jews' own feelings of happiness and relief. They clearly think that the threat is over. Of course, there remains the possibility that the Jews could be mistaken and are rejoicing prematurely, and it is this potentiality that keeps one wanting to read chapters 9–10. The reader wants to make sure that the situation turns out as well as the Jews anticipate.

Exegetical Analysis

Esther approaches Ahasuerus with her request (vv. 3-8). Her action is necessary because, in case the excitement of the previous episode has caused the reader not to notice this fact, her request has not yet been granted. Esther had asked for the salvation of the Jews as a request, but when Ahasuerus inquired about the identity of the instigator and Haman was subsequently killed, their conversation became sidetracked. Haman's death has, in actuality, solved nothing (Clines 1984a, 18). As her primary concern was never to punish Haman but to save the Jews, now Esther returns to the matter at hand. Her ultimate goal is not revenge, a destructive response, but salvation, a constructive one, and the Hebrew terminology highlights this fact. The text repeats the same verb *ḥānan*, "to seek favor," that was used when Mordecai was initially encouraging Esther to act (v. 3; cf. 4:8). Now she finally carries out that original suggestion, getting to the true purpose of her mission.

Verse 3 introduces the scene. The statement "Then Esther spoke again ... to avert the evil design of Haman the Agagite and the plot that he had devised against the Jews" provides an overview of what will happen, using indirect narration to summarize the content of Esther's direct quotation (vv. 5b-6). It also acts as a reminder. Even though Haman is dead, the narrative still reminds the reader that he was "evil" and an enemy "Agagite" and gives a bit of history ("the plot that he had devised against the Jews"). The verse provides a visual contrast as well, for as Haman was the one falling on Esther's feet to influence her a few verses ago (7:8), now she is the one falling, this time at Ahasuerus's feet.

This is the second "sceptre scene" during which Esther comes before Ahasuerus and he raises his golden sceptre to her. It is not clear whether Esther is again risking her life, as she did the first time, but if she is, the suspense is considerably heightened. The narrative invites comparison between the two scenes (cf. 5:1-5). The language of verse 4, "The king held out the golden scepter to Esther," is the same phrase in the Hebrew as at 5:2. The first time Esther came silently and regally; now, however, she comes noisily and emotionally. Other differences are evident as well. Esther's and Ahasuerus's locations are not identified, she stands after the movement of the sceptre instead of before it, and she does not wait for an extension of the sceptre to speak.

The scene is quite emotional; Esther first acts, then speaks, with great passion. Roles have changed since the previous episode. Then it was Ahasuerus who was especially ardent, but now Esther emotes while he remains calm. How to understand Esther's emotional outburst of "weeping and pleading" is not clear, and the narrative provides no hints. As she has appeared composed, almost stoic, on previous visits to Ahasuerus, her sobs and begging take the reader quite by surprise, for it is out of character for her to act in such a fashion. Is her emotion real, or is it feigned for the benefit of the king? Esther tends to employ all the means at her disposal, and if applying "feminine wiles" will get the king to do what she wants, she has no problem with doing so. Esther is not displaying weakness by crying, but within the context of her request she may be using her weeping and falling at his feet to further Ahasuerus's decision in her favor. He would not be the first man, or the last, to melt at a pretty lady's tears.

When Esther does begin to speak, she makes a more extended statement before stopping for Ahasuerus's response than she did previously (vv. 5b-6). Her rhetoric is again carefully crafted. She is polite, deprecating, and uses more conditional statements than in the past, and her persuasiveness is at its peak in this scene. Four phrases comprise her first prologue. Esther begins similarly to how she has before: "If it pleases the king" repeats her presentations at 5:4, 8 and 7:3, and "if I have won his favor" repeats 5:8 and 7:3. The last two phrases, however, are new: "if the thing seems right before the king" and "[if] I have his approval." Esther previously spoke of what was *not* suitable and advantageous to Ahasuerus (killing herself and her people [7:4]). Now she suggests what *is* suitable and proper for him to do.

Esther bases Ahasuerus's agreement on two issues, devoting two phrases to each: if he likes her and if he approves what she suggests. She covers all the bases, appealing to whether Ahasuerus likes either her or her idea, or whether it is either the good or the suitable thing to do. She uses the same Hebrew term *ṭôb,* "good," to refer both to herself and to her idea (literally "if it is good to the king" and "I am good in his eyes"), which tends to link the issues together further. Because Esther now knows without a doubt that she has his approval, she also obligates him by the manner in which she phrases the request to give his approval to her ideas. Esther's linking these two opinions together, his affection for her and his consent to her plan, places Ahasuerus in a position of having to think carefully to disengage them—a talent that is not this king's forte (Fox 2001, 93).

As she continues in verse 6, Esther speaks with great pathos and conviction. In two phrases of synonymous parallelism she no longer expresses care for her own life, but only for the lives of her "people" and her "kindred" (cf. 7:3, 4): "the calamity that is coming on my people" parallels "the destruction of my kindred." These are the people who have occupied her attention for years (2:10, 20). She presents her primary consideration as for her people and their pain, yet does so with reference to herself. Expressing the problem in solely personal terms, she rhetorically questions how she (and not they!) will be able to bear the pain of their destruction. Esther might have chosen to base her argument on moral right or wrong; that is, to explain that genocide is unethical and should not be condoned. Instead, however, she maintains that the decree should be revoked not because what Haman did was wrong, but because it upsets her. Esther forms her argument in these two verses strategically, for Ahasuerus has demonstrated that he is moved to action not so much by the evil of the plot, but by his concern for her. He has no moral sense, but what he does have is affection for her and desire that she not be troubled. It is this characteristic that Esther uses to her advantage.

Esther presents Haman as "the son of Hammedatha the Agagite" and the one who "wrote giving orders to destroy the Jews who are in all the provinces of the king" (v. 5). Continuing to place all the blame upon Haman by treating the former edict as solely his enterprise, Esther absolves Ahasuerus of his responsibility in the matter and presents the issue in a way that will seem the least personally threatening to him (cf. 7:4-6). Haman's crime is twofold: he is guilty both because of his ancestry and because of what he did. Esther implicates Haman not solely for his decree, but also for being part of an ancient tradition of enmity. This genealogical emphasis makes one wonder how much of Esther's and the Jewish community's later violence is a response to Haman himself and how much a result of a desire to avenge old wrongs.

In this environment that thrives upon the formulation of decrees, Esther's proposed solution is, not surprisingly, to write another decree. Ahasuerus has already performed a presumably much more difficult thing, executing his top official and favorite drinking buddy; convincing him to declare an edict, which he has done twice already in this story, should be a relatively easy task. Esther knows that the king's tendency is to transfer the privilege of authorship to others (1:21-22; 3:10-12). Therefore she presents her idea to him in the passive voice ("let an order be written . . ."), which provides an opening for her to write it. Esther shows herself to be a wise courtier who understands how to work with this particular ruler. She does not ask him to fix things on his own but suggests to him a viable solution, just as other courtiers (Memucan and Haman) have done. Esther has learned that it is Ahasuerus's tendency to agree to others' counsel, and she phrases her request accordingly.

The king responds in verses 7-8. That Mordecai is included as a recipient of his answer is quite surprising, as there had been no indication that he has been present during Esther's entrance and oration. Did Ahasuerus call him in? One wonders why he insists upon giving responsibility for enacting Esther's requested decree to Mordecai as well. Does Ahasuerus not trust Esther, as a woman, to do this by herself? Or does he want to involve Mordecai because he is now a royal official? Either Ahasuerus is honoring Mordecai or dishonoring Esther by including him; recalling the patriarchal nature of the court (chapters 1–2) suggests the latter option. The narrative uses an example of its typical nomenclature, in referring to "Queen Esther" and "the Jew Mordecai." At this point in the story, Esther has just revealed that she is also Jewish and Mordecai has been given a position in the royal court. Yet these facts are not here, or ever, incorporated into their names; Esther is never described by ethnicity ("the Jew Esther"), nor is Mordecai ever described by position ("the executive Mordecai"). Queenliness always remains Esther's primary identity, and Jewishness always remains Mordecai's primary identity.

Ahasuerus first reports all that he has already carried out (v. 7). He gives the sense of saying, "I've done all this already for you; what else can you want? Write it, then, instead of troubling me with it." His use of the same language ("to lay hands on") and his reminder of the same punishment as that employed for assassins and traitors (2:21) suggestively places Haman in that category as well. Ahasuerus also does not have the facts quite straight, for Haman was punished for violating the queen's life and the king's honor, not for his decree against the Jews (7:8-10). That the king blames everything on Haman reveals that he still feels no sense of his own complicity in the Jews' danger. Ahasuerus stresses that Haman is now done away with, both his reputation and his very life, and the way is now free for Esther and Mordecai to do something else. This statement reiterates the sense of 8:1-2, that the two have now replaced Haman in the administrative hierarchy.

In essence, Ahasuerus says the same thing to them as he did to Haman (3:10-11), telling them to write what seems good to them and to put it under the royal seal (v. 8). His fourfold reference to himself as "the king" stresses his own authority. His hands-off approach indicates that Ahasuerus is no more concerned about the Jewish population now than he was when Haman presented his idea for their annihilation (Bush 1996, 445). Esther earlier speaks of herself pleasing Ahasuerus (v. 5), but now he uses the same expression. Thus it no longer matters what pleases him; now it only matters to please Esther and Mordecai, and the king will rubber stamp whatever that might be. The king is becoming increasingly trusting of his officials. With Memucan, Ahasuerus himself wrote what Memucan had suggested (1:21). With Haman, he knew the general outline of what Haman would write ("a decree issued for their destruction"; 3:9). Now Ahasuerus gives free rein to Esther and Mordecai, not even knowing what they will produce ("write as you please with regard to the Jews"). They hold full responsibility for it. Moreover, the authority they are given is even greater than with previous decrees: Haman was only permitted the king's ring, but Esther and Mordecai are allowed to write "in the name of the king" as well as with "the king's ring."

This is the first reference to the irrevocable, unrepealable nature of laws formulated under royal authority. (The language at 1:19 differs.) The easiest thing to do, of course, would be to rescind the law presently on the books. Except for Darius's decree in Daniel

(Dan 6:8, 12, 15), there are no references (historical or biblical) to this characteristic of the Persian legal system, and it is historically improbable as well as logistically impractical (Moore 1971, 10-11). However, within this world of the story in which Haman's edict is immutable, the only option Esther and Mordecai have is to produce a counteredict. Mordecai figures out a way to accomplish this feat, by countering Haman's edict in small but crucial ways. In the end, Haman's decree is not revoked, as Esther asks, but is instead overwritten. Mordecai's new edict, incidentally, will also be irrevocable, so the kingdom will be left with two valid but conflicting decrees in place.

The composition and dispatch of the new decree is reported in verses 9-14. The focus shifts completely to Mordecai, as Esther is absent from the remainder of the episode; even though both she and he are commanded to write the edict, only Mordecai does so. This section is a repetition of 3:12-15, Haman's edict, using identical terms and the same events in identical sequence. The reversal of Haman's order is made very clear, as detail by detail and line by line his decree is transposed. This thorough repetition with changes made at significant points suggests that the overturning of his decree is complete, with no chance for any part of it still to hold. The sole differences of detail are the date (v. 9), that it is Mordecai who dictates it (v. 9), the particularities of the order (v. 11), and that the Jews are specifically mentioned as recipients (vv. 9, 13) along with all peoples (v. 13). (Note the useful chart with detailed comparisons in Bush 1996, 442-43.) Moreover, the three-fold terminology of "to destroy, to kill, and to annihilate" repeats Esther's very same words as well (7:4). This precise repetition makes evident to all that Mordecai has replaced Haman; the power structure in the Persian administration has been reversed.

Verse 10*b*, and verse 14*a* to a lesser extent, presents difficulties of translation with regard to the method of conveyance. The text uses rare words whose meanings are not completely known. The statement might best be rendered on the order of "And he sent out letters by the hand of runners on horses, riders on royal steeds who were the offspring of mares." There is a fine alliteration of "r" and hard "ch" sounds in the Hebrew of the final phrase (*rōkĕbê hārekeš hāʾ ăhaštĕrānîm bĕnê hārammākîm;* "riders on royal steeds who were the offspring of mares"). Therefore the rare expressions may have been chosen as much for their sound as for their meaning. Even if the specifics of the phrases in these two verses are not fully clear, the general sense of couriers sent out on speedy royal horses suffices for the sake of understanding. What remains less clear, however, is the need for such hurry; the day in question, the thirteenth of Adar, is still about nine months away.

What the Jews are allowed to do is described in verses 11-13: they are permitted to fight back and kill anyone who is against them and to take their possessions. The language is strong, and the repetition of words indicating violent actions, enmity, and vengeance adds force to the impression it gives the Jews about the behavior permitted them. The instructions pick up language that was used to describe Haman (7:6). Two terms that were used to depict him ("enemy" and "foe"; *ʾôyēb* and *ṣar*) are now used by Mordecai to describe the non-Jews ("their enemies" and "the foes" [author's translation]; *ʾōyĕbêhem* and *hāṣṣārîm;* vv. 13, 11). Now it is not only Haman who is viewed as the enemy, but also any and all non-Jews who follow his decree. As Haman is no longer alive to receive it, Mordecai transfers the Jews' anger to another subject.

It is not clear in the Hebrew text whether the "children and women" are part of the people referred to as attacking the Jews or whether they are permitted to be killed by the Jews (v. 11). In light of the parallelism with Haman's edict, in which Jewish women and children would be killed (3:13), and the fact that destroying an enemy's household was common practice in ancient warfare, the latter option is more likely. If so, the women and children suffer because of what their husbands/fathers, as heads of the household, choose to do. Haman's sons likewise lose their lives because of such a practice (9:7-10).

The reference to the Jews defending their lives reads literally "to stand for their lives" (v. 11, and also at 9:16), an expression unique to the book of Esther. Esther's own actions have paved the way for this permission. She herself has been standing before Ahasuerus (5:1; 8:5), to ask for the life of her people (7:3). Now the royal decree will go out that the Jews themselves are permitted to stand for their own lives, replicating what Esther has been doing on their behalf up until this point.

Mordecai's decree is disseminated to "every province" and "all peoples," to "every province in its own script and to every people in its own language" (vv. 9, 11). That the decree is heard by everyone, not only "the Jews in their script and their language" (v. 9), signifies that everyone knows that the Jews will fight back if and when they are attacked. This information provides a dilemma for the non-Jews of Persia. Should they obey the first command (that of Haman), attack the Jews, and thereby risk death at the Jews' hands? Or should they choose not to attack the Jews and risk punishment for disobeying a royal edict (Haman's) that is still on the books? The situation is also difficult for the Jews. They most likely would have preferred a simple annulment of Haman's decree to being placed in a position of having to decide whether to do violence to their non-Jewish neighbors and colleagues.

Reaction to the new edict is related in verses 15-17. The narrative is especially descriptive in this section, using many words where a few would suffice and illustrating both inner emotion and outer action. There are similarities to the response following the issuance of Haman's decree, although the correspondence is not as tight as between the decrees themselves. The responses of three discrete elements of the population are depicted: that of Mordecai (v. 15; cf. 4:1-2), of the Jews (vv. 16-17; cf. 4:3), and of the entire city of Susa (v. 15; cf. 3:15). All of these groups conclude the episode in a situation opposite to that in which they began. Mordecai now wears fine clothes instead of sackcloth, the city shouts and rejoices rather than experiencing distress, and the Jews rejoice and drink instead of mourn and fast.

Mordecai's going out in public in royal clothing recalls the previous time he did so, after Ahasuerus decided to reward him. This is the third instance in the book of which attention is paid to what Mordecai is wearing (4:1-4; 6:8-11; and here in v. 15). More than for any other character, the narrative is interested in what Mordecai wears; description of his clothing is not merely a fashion statement but signals important information about him at various stages of the plot. In chapter 6, the "royal robes" were borrowed, but now they are his own. Mordecai is no longer wearing someone else's royalty, reflecting someone else's high position, but now the position and the wealth are his very own and his new clothing reflects his change in circumstances.

The precise terminology used to describe this new attire echoes that of the description of the palace garden court at 1:6-7. "Blue," "white," "gold," "fine linen," and "purple" appear in both places. In chapter 1, these fine appointments were royal possessions of the king intended to impress the guests at Ahasuerus's party. That Mordecai sports the very same type of finery as does the palace itself subtly suggests that he now also symbolically belongs to the king, just like the palace curtains and royal goblets. The Hebrew term used to denote Mordecai's headgear differs from that used for the royal "crowns" (keter) worn by Vashti, Esther, and the horse (1:11; 2:17; 6:8). The term used here, 'atārah, refers more generally to a garland of some type. Whereas it occurs occasionally in the Hebrew Bible to indicate a crown worn by royalty (2 Sam 12:30 = 1 Chr 20:2; Song 3:11), it predominantly refers to a wreath or garland signifying wisdom, honor, or fine clothing (e.g., Prov 4:9; Job 19:9; Ezek 16:12; Isa 28:1, 3). Therefore, one should not understand Mordecai's golden garland as showing that he has attained royal status, but instead as a representation of his new wealth and status in the community.

The Jews respond to Mordecai's edict with great joy and celebration (vv. 16-17). The description of their reaction after Haman's edict was exterior, focusing more on their actions (4:3); this time, the emphasis is more interior, highlighting their emotions. As before, their reaction extends to "every province" (4:3). That being permitted merely to defend themselves against attack causes such joy suggests that the Jews understood Haman's command for their destruction to prohibit their own self-defense in response. The abundance and repetition of words for pleasant events and emotions—light, gladness, joy, honor, festival, holiday—emphasize that good times have come to the Jews. After everyone else has had parties galore, finally the Jews have their very own drinking party (misteh; NRSV "festival"). The phrase translated as "holiday" by the NRSV literally reads "a good day" (*yôm ṭôb;* it also appears at 9:19, 22). Used in conjunction with terms for rejoicing and partying, it suggests a time of celebration. It is of great significance that the Jews find "honor." Other characters have been so described: Ahasuerus (1:4), Persian husbands (1:20), Mordecai (6:3), and Haman and/or Mordecai (6:6, 7, 9 [twice], 11). Now, at last, it is time for the Jews to receive honor and respect.

Non-Jews respond to Mordecai's edict in two ways. First, they "shout" and "rejoice" along with the Jewish inhabitants of Susa (v. 15). But they also become afraid, and their fear is based on the Jews themselves (v. 17). The fear that Haman wanted the Jew Mordecai to have for him is now the very reaction that non-Jews have for Jews (5:9). The Jews have traversed quickly from being threatened to becoming a threat to others. The term rendered "professed to be Jews" in the NRSV is difficult to understand properly. It is a verb (*yāhad*) derived from the noun "Jew" (*yĕhudî*) and occurs only here. Possibilities for its meaning include that the people declare themselves to be Jews, or become Jews, or pose as Jews. Though any certainty of interpretation is elusive, the general populace is probably not converting to Judaism *en masse*. It is more likely that they join the Jewish side of the conflict. Recognizing that power in the government has shifted, they are aligning themselves with the faction now in authority.

Theological and Ethical Analysis

The new decree raises clear moral concerns. In the face of the senseless and cruel decree of Haman, one might wonder what improvement there is in a new regulation that counters by stating, in essence, "you can do back what is done to you." Could a better way not be found? The answer is, regrettably, no. Within the world of the story, the solution Mordecai proposes is really the only adequate option. In past generations much interpretation, often anti-semitic, of the book has misunderstood this situation, wrongly criticizing the Jews for the violence of their response. The reader must recall, however, that violence is not Esther's first choice; all she requests is the revocation of Haman's decree. But within a governmental system that cannot repeal its own laws, the only option is to enact a counterdecree. The Persian kingdom is not flexible enough in its policies to allow a nonviolent solution. Mordecai, as did Esther when choosing her methods, works as best he can within the imperfect circumstances in which he finds himself. Mordecai counters Haman's edict line for line, word for word. If he were to change even one small detail to give the Jews any benefit from their response, one could say that he crosses the line and fault him for unnecessary force. But he is careful not to do so, and his new decree merely returns the Jews to the same place they were on the morning of that day in Nisan during Ahasuerus's twelfth year (3:7). Moreover, the motivational differences between the two decrees are as revealing as the similarities (Bechtel 2002, 74-76). Haman's edict was offensive in nature, promulgated because of ethnic hatred and avarice; Mordecai's counteredict sanctions self-defense, for the goal of self-preservation.

The episode raises larger questions about the use of physical force, especially pertinent as the United States culture is statistically becoming more and more violent each year. Those who are pacifist in orientation may have difficulty in acquiescing that it is ever a proper resolution to respond to violence with violence. Yet one wonders whether it is fully appropriate for those of us who have never faced the threat of extermination, who have never experienced warfare on our own soil, even to begin to answer such ethical questions. Perhaps what determines whether it is correct to pick up pruning hook or sword (Isa 2:4; Joel 3:1-10; Mic 4:3) depends upon the circumstances.

Issues around the role and methods of women in positions of authority come to the fore. Again, the story presents a certain type of female leadership. Though Esther's chosen procedure is clearly effective within her circumstances, one should thoughtfully evaluate it before proposing it as a model for modern women's methods. A curious detail with regard to the protagonist is how quickly and completely she is eclipsed from the scene. It gives the impression that Esther (and women in general) are good for begging and pleading, but real administrative responsibilities rightfully go to Mordecai (and thereby, to men). Other courtiers—all male—also give suggestions to Ahasuerus, but they do not have to act in as placating a manner to get what they want; they do not have to cry and beg, nor do they have to base their arguments upon the king's personal affection. Even though she is queen, Esther still has to play "feminine" in this male environment, where men can simply state what they want and get it.

The constitution of minority communities remains an essential concern. Times of well-being, as·well as times of crisis, have the potential to intensify a sense of solidarity within and among peoples. Within the minority population itself, the episode presents an image of a unified Jewish community. That the Jews have maintained their own language and script indicates that they have managed to preserve their peoplehood within the challenges of the Persian multicultural environment (Berlin 2001a, 76). Relations between ethnic communities likewise continue to be significant. Whereas one might expect such a counteredict to escalate tensions among peoples, the actual result is the opposite. The vivid sense of human anguish (represented by Esther's questions to the king) is replaced by an equally vivid emotional release of danger averted. All the people of Susa rejoice, both Jew and non-Jew, in a remarkable action of solidarity; the Jews' relief is everyone's relief. Their reaction reflects the fact that when discrimination is obliterated for one group of people, it enhances not only that smaller community, but society as a whole. What benefits some, benefits all. The episode suggests that, within society, there can only be complete *shalom*, complete well-being, when all oppression is erased.

A significant criterion for multiethnic societies is the degree to which minority communities are accepted by the mainstream. Are they affirmed, or are they merely tolerated? In the story, the society's response includes not only shared emotion, but also a very change of allegiance. Non-Jews join together with Jews, choosing to align not to their own group, but with the "other." Like Ruth, they form new relationships, claim a new people as their own (Berlin 2001a, 80). While celebrating such ethnic unanimity, however, one cannot forget that we read the book of Esther after the Shoah, a time when the Gentile response, especially that of the churches in Germany and around the world, to edicts for Jewish genocide was shamefully different, more greatly resembling a confusion that fostered no widespread action or criticism (cf. 3:15). Fackenheim observes that if Gentiles had similarly sided with the Jews during the pogroms of the last century, it would have brought down the Third Reich (1990, 88). As we read the story today, it serves not only as a tribute to Jewish survival, but also as a criticism of Gentile apathy.

Theologically, one must consider the source of salvation for the Jews. In these events, deliverance does not come from God. It is not God's pronouncement that brings hope and joy; it is not God's action that delivers. Instead, it is the pronouncement of the Persian government that gives hope, an edict under the seal of a foreign king. Fruitful for theological comparison is the roughly contemporaneous account in Nehemiah 8. Ezra reads the Torah of Moses, and the people respond with celebration and rejoicing (cf. Neh 8:12, 17-18). Here in the book of Esther, however, it is not the words of YHWH but the words of Mordecai that make the people respond with such rejoicing. In the face of divine silence, human speech becomes necessary. Deliverance will come only through the Jews delivering themselves, sword to sword, fighting anyone who attacks them. In this episode, salvation is a very human endeavor, realized only through Esther's pleading, Mordecai's writing, and the people's fighting. There is no God on high who answers the people's lamentation.

THE JEWS ATTACK THEIR ENEMIES (9:1-19)

This episode reports the enactment of Mordecai's decree. The day that has been anticipated—by some with delight, by others with horror—since the throwing of the lot eleven months ago has finally arrived. The Jews do battle against those who attack them, Esther requests a second day of fighting in Susa, and there is celebration at the culmination of their defense.

Literary Analysis

From this point until the conclusion of the book, the literary style changes somewhat. The narrative flow of the first eight chapters is interrupted by a series of summarizing reports throughout this episode. The various sections of the narrative are not well integrated and it is difficult to determine how the material connects together. Nor is the episode as suspenseful as previous scenes have been, for the result of the clash between Haman's and Mordecai's edicts is given in the very first verse (v. 1). Moreover, the sequence and details in the two Greek versions of the story vary considerably from the Hebrew version. These facts have led some interpreters to believe that this final portion of the story, chapters 9–10, is one or even two secondary additions to the original story (cf. Torrey 1944; Loewenstamm 1971; Clines 1984a, 39-63; Dorothy 1997, 266-75, 313-20). Yet there are also significant literary, thematic, and textual connections between the ending and the previous chapters (cf. Berg 1979, 39-47, 103-13; Fox 1991, 99-126; Jobes 1996, 195-221; Fried 2000). The issue of the ending of the book is complex and not easily resolved.

In this section the bias of the narrator emerges more strongly. The narrative voice is not as disinterested as it has been throughout the earlier part of the book, but is now very clearly on the side of the Jews. This report, indeed, comes across much like wartime propaganda, giving an unrealistically positive spin on the situation. It recounts events in simplistic and glowing, even hyperbolic, terms. Surely 75,810 fatal injuries to the enemy could not be achieved without injury to the Jews, yet no casualties are admitted. The closest the narrative comes to revealing details of the combat itself is the mention that it occurs by means of swords (v. 5). Everything is neat and tidy; there is no blood, no gore, no agony described.

The action occurs over the course of three days, the thirteenth through the fifteenth of Adar. Great attention is given to temporal details throughout the episode, on what days events occur. Two distinct locales comprise the setting: the city and citadel of Susa and the outlying provinces of the kingdom. The battle outcome and resultant celebration parallel each other in these two locations but are described separately according to the dates of the events. The general, kingdom-wide response to Mordecai's decree is provided first, in verses 1-4. Verse 3 serves as a summary statement about the battle activities in general, which are elaborated throughout the remainder of the episode. The particularities of the fighting are then provided, first what happens in Susa (vv. 6-15) and then what happens in the outer provinces (vv. 16-17).

Esther and Ahasuerus play secondary roles in the episode, and Mordecai receives a brief mention. The focus here is upon the Jewish people. The Jews are presented as acting as a group, with no one individuated. This is the third time that the Jews' actions have been noted: first, when they mourned and fasted (4:3, 16) and then when they rejoiced (8:16-17). This third description, that of the Jews when they fight, is the most extended view of them in the book.

Exegetical Analysis

The episode begins in verse 1 with a summary of events thus far and the repetition of a date that has been noted twice before (3:13; 8:12). This summary speaks of "the king's command" but does not specify whether it is Haman's edict or Mordecai's edict. As both were promulgated under the king's seal (3:10, 12; 8:8, 10), either is a valid possibility, though Haman's decree seems more likely in the context of the rest of the verse. The comment that it is "the very day when the enemies of the Jews hoped to gain power over them, but which had been changed to a day when the Jews would gain power over their foes" expresses the completeness of the reversal by using the same terminology in both phrases but transposing the subject and the object of the action of "gaining power" (v. 1). It stresses that what happens is the exact opposite of what was planned. Though reversals have been implicit throughout the preceding events, here they are finally made explicit. The text reads, literally, "but it was overturned." In one sense this brief phrase, a mere two words in Hebrew *(wĕnahăpôk hû')*, serves to sum up the point of the entire book (Levenson 1997, 8-9, 119).

The expression that the non-Jews "sought [the Jews'] ruin" seems too strong an assessment, as the general populace has not visibly displayed any animosity to this point (v. 2). If they do choose to attack the Jews, it would be more likely as a result of obedience to a royal (Haman's) decree. The Jews' response, ironically, is described as "to lay hands on" *(lišlōḥ yād)*, the same expression used for the assassins', and then for Haman's, intentions (2:21; 3:6; 8:7). The ramifications of this action are universal, the Jews gathering in *all* the provinces and *all* peoples being afraid. Just as permissions went out to every province (8:9, 13), now the Jews in all those provinces know how to act on that day. These happenings have the same universal ramifications as anticipated from Vashti's actions, which also was to affect "all the peoples" and "all the provinces" (1:16), although instead of instability in individual marriages the result is now instability in Persian society as a whole.

The non-Jews experienced fear after the announcement of Mordecai's decree (8:17). Now, these nine months later, they are still afraid. Indeed, during this interim period they have become more frightened rather than less so; then only "many of the peoples" were afraid but now "all peoples" are fearful (v. 2). Yet this fear now causes people to respond differently to the Jews. Then, out of their fear, the people sided with the Jews, perhaps even intending to help defend them against those non-Jews who would decide to attack. Now this same fear does not spur them to act but signifies that their defeat is certain. Although their earlier fear led to action, this present fear leads to paralysis ("no one could withstand them"), or at least their inability to defend themselves effectively against the Jews.

Verse 3 reflects a reversal of political power as well as of brute physical power (who slaughters whom). Included in the list of individuals who choose to support the Jews is a group literally described as "the doers of work which was the king's" (*'ōśê hammělā'kâ 'ăšer lammelek;* author's translation). This phrase most likely refers to mid-level bureaucrats, in contrast to the variety of officials, satraps, and governors at higher levels of administration. If so, it gives the sense that, from high to low, a diversity of types and ranks of people endorse the Jews. The individuals who are given charge to put Haman's bribe into the royal treasury are named similarly, "doers of the work" (*'ōśê hammělā'kâ,* 3:9; author's translation). If they are the same people, their new allegiance to Mordecai, away from Haman, is particularly significant.

Noted in these two verses (vv. 2-3) is both fear of the Jews and fear specifically of Mordecai. The general population ("all peoples") would know only the decree and not that Mordecai was the one behind it, for it was disseminated under Ahasuerus's name. Therefore, the object of their dread is the Jews in general, mentioned in that decree (8:11, 13). The government administrators listed in verse 3, in contrast, know that it was really Mordecai who was behind that decree, and therefore they base their alarm upon him specifically. All these government employees are the ones who know to support the Jews, which means that those persons who do not support the Jews and choose to attack them, and are subsequently killed, are not government-affiliated people. Those in the realm of the official Persian administration are more savvy as to where the power now lies, with Esther and Mordecai, and choose to side with them. Those who are outside the administration do not have this perspective, this insider information. And they pay for their lack of information with their lives.

The action is described with vividness (v. 5). The sword, slaughter, and destruction provide a portrait of the scene, a sense of bloodshed and carnage all around. The sense of totality established in verses 2-3 continues; the Jews kill "all their enemies." If everyone is killed, then, the final death count must be the number of those non-Jews who decide to attack. Yet the text, oddly, includes no mention of the non-Jews attacking first, but only the Jews' attack: it leaves a gap for the reader to wonder whether the Jews' action is indeed defensive or might possibly be offensive. The description in verse 16, however, more explicitly suggests a defensive action in the provinces, and perhaps this portrayal can be understood universally for all the fighting.

Verses 7-10 report how Haman's sons are also killed in the fighting. With this occurrence, all of the reasons for Haman's pride—position, money, and children—are now done away with (Fox 2001, 110). All of the sons' names are listed, though such a roster seems rather unnecessary, as the only function they serve in the story is to be dead. This treatment mirrors other lists of names of persons from chapter 1 who also have no independent action (the eunuchs at 1:10, the officials at 1:14). If one understands 8:11 as permitting the Jews to attack children and women, here they indeed do so. As the sons themselves have not acted along with their father against the Jews or Mordecai, one may wonder why it is necessary that they die as well.

In this section Mordecai is the focus, first as an object of fear (v. 3) and then as a man of reputation (v. 4). The Hebrew term used to describe Mordecai is *gādôl,* literally "great" (translated as "powerful" in the NRSV). This greatness can be in terms of honor or importance, not necessarily of raw political power. The best way to think of his increasing greatness is that Mordecai is now distinguished, as report of him travels throughout the land. The attribute of reputation is important in ancient culture. As the story progresses, Mordecai receives greater and greater attention. He was first in the public eye when receiving his reward from Ahasuerus (6:10-11), then he was further recognized by the queen and king when given oversight of Haman's household and Ahasuerus's ring (8:2). Now he receives recognition from others, too. Mordecai's initial power in the realm of the palace administration now grows to recognition throughout the entire kingdom. As verse 4 is an extension of verse 3, this acknowledgment appears to be more by those officials in remote areas of the kingdom than (most likely) by the general population throughout the provinces. The reason for Mordecai's reputation is not stated: does he gain fame because he wrote this decree, or has he performed other actions of note in the intervening nine months as well? With this characteristic, Mordecai resembles other biblical characters whose influence and reputation increase as time progresses; e.g., Judith, Daniel, and Joseph, though more specific reasons are given for their advancements in power and prestige.

Common elements unite the summaries of the various incidents of fighting throughout the episode. The reports note that the Jews gather and fight, that they kill x number of enemies but do not take plunder. The act of gathering embodies their defense as a group rather than individually (vv. 2, 15, 16, 18). The Jews apparently do not anticipate that individual non-Jews will attack individual Jews, but that the non-Jews will mount an orchestrated and united attack. Therefore, they respond in kind. The Jews now act not as an ethnic or religious group, as when they gathered to fast and to mourn together (4:3, 16), but as a military group, an army.

Not "touching" the non-Jews' possessions echoes the language used for their actions toward the non-Jews in general; they physically "lay hands" (v. 2) upon people but not upon plunder (vv. 10, 15, 16). That the Jews are permitted to take plunder (8:11) but do not do so shows a morally positive side to their attack. As this detail is repeated thrice, the narrative emphasizes that the Jews are not trying to benefit financially from this conflict. This detail also provides a contrast with the story of King Agag, Haman's ancestor (3:1; 8:5). The story in 1 Samuel 15 records how, in battle with Agag and the Amalekites, Saul *does* take plunder even though doing so is in direct violation of YHWH's instructions. In the present altercation the Jews do the opposite; correcting the failure of their ancestors, their choice will "wipe away the stain of the greed of the Israelites who defeated the Amalekites in Saul's time" (Fox 2001, 115).

At four instances the narrative reports the number of victims: five hundred in Susa (vv. 6, 12) and 75,000 in the rest of the territory (v. 16) on the thirteenth of Adar; three hundred in Susa on the fourteenth of Adar (v. 15). For the Susan casualties, the narrative uses the Hebrew term ʾîš. Although ʾîš signifies "man" in its primary meaning, it can also mean more generally "person" as well. In this instance, it should be understood according to its predominant meaning, indicating that it is men who are killed in the combat, not the women and children mentioned at 8:11. Similarly, men can be understood at verse 16, in which a masculine plural participle, "those who hated them" *(bĕśōnĕʾêhem)*, is used to refer to the persons killed in the outlying territories. As a result of the fighting, the wives of all these men will become widowed and all their children will become fatherless. One cannot help but wonder what will happen to the women and their children after the loss of their support, their husbands and their sons. The earlier fear was that wives would talk back to their husbands (1:17-18). Yet how much worse is the present situation for individual families throughout the Persian kingdom.

The next section describes what occurs to bring about the action in Susa on the fourteenth of Adar (vv. 11-15). Ahasuerus's and Esther's conversation provides an interlude to the battlefield action (vv. 12-14a). Report of the day's fighting is first made to Ahasuerus, literally, "the letter came to the king" (v. 11). The Hebrew term meaning "letter" *(sēper)* is the same term used to designate Memucan's letters (1:22), Haman's letters (3:13; 8:5), and Mordecai's letters (8:10). One sees a shift in the direction of information throughout the empire. These other letters have all gone *out* from the palace to the kingdom; now, however, the flow of information has reversed, as a document comes *in* to the palace from the outside.

Ahasuerus apparently assumes that Esther does not know what had happened in Susa, so he tells her. The seeming pleasure or admiration he evidences when reporting the massive death toll of his people strikes one as incongruous; it furthers his characterization as foolhardy and disconnected from the Persian citizenry. This scene is another petition and request scene, the fourth and final one in the book (cf. 5:1-8; 7:1-10; 8:3-8). This time Ahasuerus initiates the conversation, coming to Esther first and speaking first. The phrasing and terminology about the granting of petitions and fulfilling of requests is precisely the same as before, but this conversation is considerably more abbreviated. Giving her unrestricted opportunity, he does not limit her gift to half the kingdom but says merely "it shall be fulfilled," and she uses only a single qualifying "if it please the king" before telling him her request. These two individuals have gone through this routine before; they know the drill and need not rehearse it again. Ahasuerus's inclusion of "further" indicates that he views Esther's present request as something new, but why he assumes that Esther desires something more is not clear. He has already granted the request she finally revealed, which was to write a new decree (8:5). If Esther is not expecting to be asked to provide another request, she nonetheless is able to think on her feet and comes up with a reply on the spot.

What Esther requests is actually two things: permission for the Jews to repeat that day's action tomorrow and a hanging (or impaling) of the bodies of Haman's sons. One might wonder *why*

Esther wants these things. What benefit does she foresee from more death? After all, the Jews of Susa have already had their chance that day. In an honor-shame culture such as this one, the public hanging for Haman's sons is more understandable, if first assuming that they deserved death in the first place. Death would not be fully satisfactory; they must go the way of their father and undergo public shaming. But her desire for further death for the general population makes Esther appear opportunistic, even vindictive. By asking for another day she surpasses Haman's original decree, which was only for one day (the thirteenth of Adar). The non-Jews have no royal decree demanding that they attack on the fourteenth.

In this episode, Esther appears at her most authoritative. This is the case, first, because unlike their previous encounters, Ahasuerus comes to her to initiate conversation. Then her request is carried out promptly (v. 14). Although Esther's previous request was also readily granted, Mordecai was then permitted to take over (8:5-8). Here Mordecai is not involved at all; she is the one to take command and the king responds to her directive. Second, Esther presents herself in a more regal and restrained fashion. This time there are no tears, no pleading, no equivocating, no melodramatic confessions, but Esther states simply and forthrightly what she wants. It is ironic that it is Mordecai of whom the non-Jews are afraid, and not Esther (v. 3). As queen, Esther still holds a higher position than he. Moreover, she also shows herself to be more dangerous, more lethal to the non-Jews; her request for an extra day's fighting leads to the death of three hundred of their men.

Esther's request is realized in verses 14-15. Her decree is simply reported as enacted ("done"). This time there is no description of how it came about or details about how it is disseminated, as was the case for the edicts of Memucan, Haman, and Mordecai (1:19-22; 3:10-15; 8:8-14). Both of the elements of the action on the thirteenth of Adar are paralleled here: destruction of hundreds and harm to Haman's progeny (vv. 5-10). There is, however, an odd discrepancy in the reports of the proceedings. The Jews reportedly kill *all* their enemies on the first day of fighting in Susa (v. 5). If that is the case, where do these additional men come from, so that they are available for the Jews to kill them on the second day? After hearing of the first day's report of five hundred casualties, one doubts that three hundred of the men who had supported the Jews the first day (cf. v. 3) wake up the next morning and decide to change their allegiance.

One must consider the situation of Zeresh at the conclusion of all these events: she is left completely bereft. Her financial means were taken and she was shamed by having her husband publicly hanged in her front yard (7:9–8:2). Now her sons are killed, dashing any hopes she might have had for future financial stability, and she is further shamed through their hanging. In and of themselves, these actions could be considered unjust and cruel. But the further irony of her situation is that she is the first non-Jew to take the Jewish side in this altercation, and she is the first one to recognize the power of Mordecai (6:13).

The latter part of the episode becomes repetitive. The activities of the Jews in the provinces are reported, how they gather, kill, and celebrate (vv. 16-17), then the similar actions and sequence of the Jews in Susa (v. 18). The episode concludes with a summary statement about how the Jews in the territories celebrate (v. 19). Even though battle statistics of five hundred and then three hundred are understandable (vv. 6, 15), it is hard to imagine—and perhaps hard to believe as well—the destruction of 75,000 men. Death of this magnitude would have decimated the Persian population. The grand death toll represents another instance of the hyperbolic style of this narrative. The sequence occurs over two days, the thirteenth and fourteenth of Adar, for the country Jews, and over three days, the thirteenth, fourteenth, and fifteenth of Adar, for the Susan Jews. In so doing, the Jews follow a sequence as old as creation, of work followed by rest (Gen 2:2-3). It is very possible that the events are presented in this way to reflect variant current traditions about Purim. The second day of fighting in Susa may therefore be an etiological detail included by the author to explain why different communities of Jews celebrate Purim on different days, some on the fourteenth day and some on the fifteenth day of the month.

In their celebrations, the Jews repeat the same types of action as they did after the writing of Mordecai's decree (8:16-17): they are filled with gladness and they hold more drinking parties. Now they (at least the Jews in the villages; v. 19) also give to others; they do not celebrate only amongst themselves but also look outward, sharing their happiness and good fortune. In the phrase "a holiday on which they send portions to one another" (author's translation), it is not exactly clear what it is that the people exchange. The Hebrew term *mānâ* usually indicates a portion of offering given to priests and temple workers (e.g., 2 Chr 31:3, 19; Lev 7:33; Neh 12:44, 47). In one other instance in the Hebrew Bible the term denotes the sending of gifts on a holy day to persons who are needy (Neh 8:10, 12), which is a similar context to its use here in verse 19 and later at 9:22. Therefore, this action appears to reflect a festival custom that might have developed during early Judaism.

Theological and Ethical Analysis

This episode represents the most challenging section of the book for theological interpretation. The language is strong and divisive, emphasizing enmity and destruction. The scene is bloody, the ground throughout all the territory of the kingdom strewn with thousands of dead bodies. The violence decreed in the previous episode is here carried out. Even though massive in nature, the fighting still adheres to the regulations spelled out in Mordecai's edict. One must recall that the Jews are only allowed to act in self-defense, not in revenge; they are not permitted to initiate any of the fighting, but merely to defend themselves if they are attacked. This fact indicates, consequentially, that the number of non-Jews who are killed is the number who decide, following Haman's edict, to attack Jews. The action is indeed violent, but it is a controlled and orderly violence—no guerilla attacks, no marauding mobs that easily could have evolved instead. It is also stressed how the Jews refuse to take plunder, thereby publicly demonstrating that they are choosing to fight with integrity and not seeking any benefit from their enemies' defeat. Readers may not agree that violence is the optimum way to solve disputes but still must respect the Jews' choice to act honorably within the situation they are given. In warfare there can be a moral sense, a right and a wrong way to fight—and the Jews choose the former. In all, one cannot condone the violence that pervades the conclusion of the story, but is left only to mourn the fact that it is necessary for self-preservation in a world in which enemies abound (Crawford 1999, 934).

A puzzling aspect to this episode is how to understand Esther's request for another day's fighting in Susa. Is this claim not excessive and unwarranted force? Not necessarily, as the second day's fighting still must fall under the original edict, and therefore be in self-defense only. Bechtel argues that Esther's request is consistent with her overall goal for Jewish safety and with her previous characterization as a wise leader (2002, 79-80). The fact that Esther's action in this episode is often strongly criticized, that she is frequently faulted as bloodthirsty and vindictive, reflects a gender bias in interpretation. Women, in general, are often expected to be only gentle in spirit and demeanor; physical force is considered somehow unladylike and even antithetical to the female psyche. This prejudice is the same double standard that causes some persons to argue that a woman should never become president, because she would not be able to press that red button, she would balk at sending a nation into war. The present action of Esther (along with her biblical counterparts Deborah, Jael, Judith, and Delilah) suggests that such sexist assumptions are unfounded.

The most ambiguous detail of the episode is the death of the ten sons of Haman. Of course, the reader is not told the children's ages, to know whether they are old enough to be agents in the fighting. Yet they have never been presented as followers of their father's hateful ways, so one cannot assume their guilt. Perhaps it is considered too risky to Jewish safety to allow them to live, that Haman's legacy needs to be completely obliterated; perhaps their death reflects the biblical injunction to eliminate Amalekites (cf. Exod 17:8-16; Deut 25:17-19); or perhaps it nullifies Haman's pride in the large number of his sons (5:11). Nonetheless, for whatever reason they are killed, this detail presents children murdered because of the guilt of the parent, a fact that makes one interpreter judge this passage to be "unsalvageable" (Fackenheim 1990, 92). These sons represent the fact that warfare too often includes what is euphemistically termed collateral damage, civilian as well as military casualties.

The episode raises the question of how we are to live with persons who are not like us. The picture is that of an unstable society that is at odds with itself. In the midst of the non-Jews there is division. Those who fear, support the Jews; those who hate, fight the Jews. Their emotional responses—either fear or hate—divide the population. Whereas fear of their leaders and their neighbors is understandable under the circumstances, governance by terror rather than by justice is never a good long-term solution for a stable community. Language of open hostility runs throughout the episode: "enemies of the Jews," "foes," "those who hated them" is the terminology used for the non-Jews who choose to attack the Jews. These Gentiles seem unable to find a better way to live with others than to assail those who are unlike themselves. An unanswered question is why so very many people dislike the Jews so much that they risk their own lives to attack them. But, as Fox observes, "the explanation for antisemitism resides within the antisemite's soul, and the narrator's refraining from giving further motivation for this irrational behavior is realistic" (2001, 111). The sheer number of casualties reveals the grand nature of the problem in the Persian kingdom, that the underground reservoir of animos-ity runs deep. All the ethnic tension that surfaces in the episode should be seen as a warning to any civilization. It reflects a situation that a society would never experience unless it succors its Hamans, unless it gives credence to prejudice and discrimination.

The number of fatalities is an example of a disproportionate "overkill." Throughout the story there has been an overabundance of almost everything—of wine, of women, of servants, of advisors, of provinces, of draperies. And now there is an overabundance of corpses. To take the large death toll literally, as any more morally significant than any of the other exaggerated elements, is to misread the story. The most appropriate way to understand the carnage is to consider the social function such literature plays. Craig's classification of the story according to the genre of carnivalesque is imminently useful at this point. A culture's production and use of carnivalesque literature has a social function, serving as renewal, part of a life-giving cycle for the community. All carnival literature necessarily includes death. It is not simple dying, however, but death that leads to a rebirth of some type (1995, 120-36). As carnivalesque literature developed from the people's response to oppressive forces from political authorities, so future generations who also face authoritarian regimes will benefit when reading the Esther story. This fantasy victory functions as a safety valve, facilitating emotional release and permitting Jews to trust the security and continuance of their community (Berlin 2001a, 82). When faced with the oppressive situations that minority communities will inevitably face, the story's over-the-top farce of massive casualties for the oppressor can help provide an outlet for their real-life frustration. The purpose for the slaughter at the end of the book is not because it did happen, but so that it *does not* happen. It functions to prevent violence rather than to glorify it.

THE ESTABLISHMENT OF PURIM (9:20–10:3)

This final episode brings to a close the book of Esther. It includes information about two new letters that are written and dispatched, one by Mordecai alone and the other with Esther, legislating the observance of Purim. The narrative summarizes the foregoing events of the story and concludes with a note describing Mordecai's prestige in the kingdom.

Literary Analysis

This episode focuses upon Mordecai, Esther, and the Jews. Ahasuerus no longer plays an active role. Although the overall topic is the authorization of a new Jewish holiday, this section of the book reads like a hodgepodge of action and information. The account is no longer in the smooth, linear style of the story to this point; the emphasis, to even a greater degree than that of the previous episode, is as much upon summarization as upon narration. The episode might best be divided into sections as follows: Mordecai's instructions for an annual celebration (9:20-23); a selective summary of events and an admonition to observe Purim (9:24-28); Esther and Mordecai's good wishes and another admonition to observe Purim (9:29-32); and an overview about Mordecai's continuing influence (10:1-3).

Three themes help hold the episode together: writing, establishing, and time. Writing has been an important motif throughout the story as a whole, but here attention upon writing is more greatly concentrated. Nothing is left to the realm of oral tradition, as the narrative emphasizes how everything is written down for the sake of people both current and future (9:20, 23, 26, 27, 29, 30, 32; 10:2). The action of authorizing and establishing customs is also highlighted. The sevenfold repetition of the Hebrew verb *qûm*, "to establish," makes certain that the reader will not miss this point (9:21, 27, 29, 31 [thrice], 32). Correspondingly, the Jews obligingly take on the directives imposed by their leaders, adopting their suggestions for the new customs (9:23, 27). The narrative also includes the theme of time. It is important not merely that specific deeds be performed, but that they also be done at the proper times, on the legislated days (9:21, 27, 31). The narrator both looks back in time, recalling the origin and spread of festival celebrations, and looks forward to the festival's continual celebration into the future (Berlin 2001a, 91).

Exegetical Analysis

Mordecai's establishment of Purim customs is recounted in 9:20-23. The sequence is the same as in previous directives: an official writes a missive, it is sent throughout the land, and the population does what it commands. Mordecai replicates the established procedure of the Persian government, though now with regard to the Jewish community. First, however, he chronicles what has occurred (9:20). Now the Jews will have a record of a significant event in their history, just as the Persians have (6:1). Mordecai himself now acts as a scribe as he, and not the royal secretaries, writes the account (cf. 3:12; 8:9). The absence of palace intermediaries presents Mordecai as more personally involved in this endeavor. This letter is not to be received by everyone in the kingdom, by all peoples in their own languages, as past letters have been (1:21-22; 3:12; 8:9), but is directed to a specific ethnic population, the Jews. Yet within the Jewish population, distribution is complete. This breadth is with regard to both people ("all Jews") and place ("all the provinces of King Ahasuerus, both near and far"). Though the inclusion of all provinces has occurred numerous times throughout the story, the additional designation of "near and far" is new (cf. 1:16, 22; 2:3; 3:8, 12, 13, 14; 4:3; 8:9, 11, 12, 13, 17; 9:2, 4). Every single person in every single locale—that is, absolutely every Jew in Persia—is told to enact these new customs.

Mordecai links the projected customs to the actual events. He introduces a few changes, though, most particularly expanding the period of the celebration (9:21). As the incidents occurred, fighting took place on the thirteenth day of the month of Adar (or the thirteenth and fourteenth in Susa) and celebrating on the fourteenth day (or the fifteenth in Susa) (9:16-18). Celebrating, therefore, was a single-day affair. In contrast, in the future the Jews will celebrate for two days, the fourteenth and the fifteenth of the month. (It is also possible, however, that 9:21 may instead indicate that the respective communities should continue their celebrations on the dates they currently observe, either the fourteenth *or* the fifteenth.) The shift in emotion, "from sorrow into gladness and from mourning into a holiday," is a direct reference to the emotions recorded in the story proper, from the sorrow following Haman's decree (4:1-3) to the joy following Mordecai's decree (8:15-17). It represents a full and total reversal of emotional state. The term used for "mourning" is from the same uncommon Hebrew root *('ābal)* that designates Haman's mourning after he paraded Mordecai through the city (6:12). The repetition of this term plays up the differing fates of Haman and the Jews. Haman's mourning, in the end, is never converted to joy; the Jews' mourning, which was caused by Haman, is replaced by a happiness that Haman will never experience.

The Jews thus begin the custom of Purim. Throughout the story there has been much partying for varied purposes: to show off (1:1-8); to celebrate (2:18; 3:15; 8:17); and to persuade (5:4-8;

7:1-10). The partying during Purim, as it continues into the future, will have commemoration as its purpose, to cause people to remember their heritage. The phrase "the Jews adopted as a custom what they had begun to do" may refer to their initial celebration immediately upon their victory (9:17-19), or it may signify that the Jews had already begun a customary celebration prior to Mordecai's writing down formal and official regulations to so do (9:23). In their Purim remembrances the Jews are asked to recall two elements. They are to reenact the original emotions (the "gladness") and the original actions (the engaging in drinking parties and giving of portions). Mordecai's command turns these elements from a one-time occurrence into a repeated reenactment of the original fighters' actions. The Jews are not, as one might expect, to celebrate their martial victory, but instead their relief and rest following the victory; it is not revenge that will continue to be reenacted, but deliverance. The new regulations go beyond the original circumstances when introducing the action of "sending ... presents to the poor" in addition to the giving of portions the Jews originally performed (9:19). Just as is the case with other feast days on which Jews give to the poor (cf. Neh 8:10-12; Tob 2:2), generosity will henceforth be built into the Purim festival. The Jews' partying will incorporate an altruistic element. It represents the only partying in the story whose purpose lies not only in the revelers' own enjoyment, but also in benefiting others.

A further admonition to keep Purim, preceded by a summary statement, comprises the second section of the episode (9:24-28). This digest (9:24-25) is a great condensation of events, especially notable for its changed presentation of what happened, differing in terminology and in detail. It is not clear whose perspective this summary represents, but it is possible that it presents an encapsulation of "these things" that Mordecai includes in his letter (9:20). If this is the case, the differences from the preceding narrative may be deliberate (Bush 1996, 480-81). Haman is now credited with wanting not only to "destroy" the Jews as before (7:4; 8:5), but also to put them into a panic. The sense of the Hebrew verb *hāmam*, translated as "crush" in the NRSV, is more precisely "to worry" or "to confuse." The choice of this term makes a wordplay with the name "Haman." It is frequently used to describe action in wartime, and typically God is the one who throws people into their state of confusion (e.g., Exod 14:24; Josh 10:10; Judg 4:15; 1 Sam 7:10). That Haman does so instead reflects the interest of the book as a whole on the human realm rather than on the divine. Haman, therefore, is now charged with affecting the Jews not only physically (by killing), but also mentally.

Divergences in plot details abound in 9:25. As the Hebrew text has only the third-person feminine singular pronoun to designate who or what came before the king, it is unclear whether Esther or the plot (from 9:24) is intended. If Esther is meant, as the NRSV understands the referent to the pronoun, this summary gives the impression that Haman's death and his sons' hanging were both accomplished in the same conversation between Esther and Ahasuerus, whereas in the story Esther twice "came before the king" (7:1-10; 9:11-14). It also presents Haman and the sons as being hanged at the same time. Ahasuerus is now given credit for determining to punish these men; whereas, in truth, neither the sons' killing nor their hanging were his ideas; they originated with the Jews and Esther, respectively. Moreover, Ahasuerus put nothing in writing with regard to Haman. It was only written—and that through Mordecai—that the Jews might defend themselves, but by then Haman was long dead. The injunction for his hanging was by oral command only. Furthermore, the events are retold in such a way as to emphasize Haman's guilt. The threefold repetition in these two verses of the Hebrew word ḥāšab, "to plot," makes him appear especially sinister. And as Haman's culpability is accentuated, Mordecai's responsibility is forgotten; this statement neglects the fact that Mordecai, not the Jews in general, was Haman's primary enemy.

In sum, this synopsis in 9:25 is a fine example of selective reporting. It is a reinterpretation of the events from a particular point of view—some details emphasized, other details de-emphasized or omitted. This statement reframes the past incidents as centered on ethnic animosity rather than on a conflict between individual courtiers with ethnic tensions only as a general backdrop. The perspective of this retelling of the previous events noticeably differs from the perspective of the narration in chapters 5–8; the story is not merely summarized, but actively reframed in this brief synopsis.

An etiological statement explains first how the festival of Purim received its name, and second, why the Jews observe this festival (9:26). There is little logic in deriving the name "Purim" from Haman's lot, and the name of the holiday probably existed before the book's composition (cf. Fox 2001, 120-21; Levenson 1997, 128). The term *pūrīm* is grammatically plural, in contrast to the grammatically singular *pūr*, and the earlier statement including this term (3:7) is most likely an insertion by a later editor. The reference to "this letter" must be to Mordecai's letter establishing the holiday. The Jews are presented as agreeing to celebrate Purim for two reasons: they rely upon outside command ("because of all that was written in this letter"), and they rely upon their own experience (because "of what they had faced in this matter, and of what had happened to them"; 9:26). Thus, the Jews are merging their personal experience with outside information. They do not decide to follow everything in Mordecai's writing just because he says to do it; it must also correspond with their own experience and their own wisdom.

When and by whom Purim is to be celebrated is the focus of 9:27-28. A list of three categories of people is given: "themselves," "their descendants," and "all who joined them" (v. 27). The terminology of the last designation is vague. Does it signify that the Jews welcome non-Jews to celebrate along with them, like those who sided with the Jews in the conflict (8:17; 9:3)? Or does it signify actual conversion? That these people celebrate Purim and are linked with Jewish descendants makes the latter more probable. These three phrases indicate that both the current Jewish population ("themselves") and those who will comprise the Jewish community in the future ("their descendants and all who joined them") are to commemorate Purim faithfully. Four designations of people are named as 9:28 continues, all of whose members are to observe the festival: generation, family, province, city. In the syntax of the Hebrew text, these four terms are presented in parallel fashion. The first two (generation, family) indicate social groups, and the last two (province, city) indicate places, both rural and urban. This combination provides a universal sense to Purim celebration; every social group in every place will observe the festival. Not only by whom but also *when* Purim is celebrated is of concern. Precision, punctuality, and regularity are of great importance: "these two days ... at the time appointed." This concluding warning in 9:28 is quite strong. Observance dare not be neglected or forgotten, no matter how many generations removed from Esther's and Mordecai's actions.

In the third section of this episode, Esther and Mordecai write and dispatch a document about Purim, the fifth and final letter in the book (9:29-32). Because of the repetitive nature and the textual inconsistencies of these verses, it is difficult to sort out the various actors (for a fuller discussion of the complexities, consult Day 1995, 158-64). This is the "second letter" regarding the festival; the first was Mordecai's letter (9:20-23). The two cousins now write about other issues pertaining to Purim and to wish the Jews well. It is the first action that Esther and Mordecai actually do together, as all of their previous efforts to bring salvation to the Jews were performed by either one or the other individually. Though once given the opportunity to work with Esther as a team, Mordecai took all the responsibility upon himself (8:7-14). Now Esther also has occasion to author a document for general consumption. There is great irony in the fact that the very first letter in the story was composed specifically to keep women from having too much power (1:13-22), but now it is a woman who is writing the final command. Esther's transformation from sexual to political queen is now complete; "when she is signing edicts and improving the lot of the Jews, there are no details about what Esther wears, how she smells, or who is looking at her" (Bach 1997, 199). This action demonstrates that women's power can have a positive influence throughout Persia, instead of the feared negative kingdom-wide influence of Vashti.

The initial verse in this section (9:29) is an overview statement that summarizes what will be explicated in the following three verses (9:30-32). Unlike Haman's paternal parentage, which is repeated frequently throughout the story (3:1; 8:3, 5; 9:10, 24), this is only the second instance that Esther's father is named. The narrative notes her lineage when this character is first introduced (2:15), and now at the last time she is seen. Likewise, 9:30 repeats a detail from the beginning of the story that has not been included when speaking of the provinces ("the one hundred twenty-seven provinces of the kingdom of Ahasuerus," cf. 1:1). These repetitions serve to link the conclusion of the story to its introduction, giving the book a sense of completion and symmetry.

Mordecai, by himself, is the one who actually sends out this letter (9:30). The Hebrew text reads "and he [Mordecai] sent letters to all the Jews . . ."; the verb "to send" is a third-person masculine singular form (author's translation). Esther and Mordecai work jointly on the tasks necessary to produce and disseminate this information, each having primary responsibility for individual duties. Esther commands (9:32) and composes (9:29); Mordecai dispatches (9:30). As he has sent out a letter before, he would be familiar with the official procedure (8:9-14). Esther and Mordecai perform parallel actions: he first writes to the Jews (9:20-23), and now she does. Both of these letters establish customs about Purim ("these days of Purim should be observed") and stress that it is to be celebrated by the Jewish community at certain times ("at their appointed times") now and into the future ("for themselves and for their descendants"; 9:31). Yet the letters' focus also differs. Mordecai's instructions about Purim require only joy and happy celebration (9:22). Esther's letter instead focuses upon memorial fasts and acts of mourning ("regulations concerning their fasts and their lamentations"). It is a more solemn mandate, requiring abstinence and penitence. The purpose, along with establishing commemorative practices, is to give good tidings and encouragement to the people, "wishing peace and security to all the Jews" (9:30). These are both concerns that Esther has demonstrated before. She insisted upon the Jews' fasting in the midst of their difficulties (4:16), and she also has shown herself to have great sympathy for the Jews and concern for their well-being (7:3-4; 8:5-6). Not writing only to command, Esther, along with Mordecai, wishes her people well. Esther shows herself to be a benevolent monarch.

That Esther's writing is referred to as a "command" *(ma'ămār)* highlights her growth in maturity and authority (9:32). This term has been used earlier in the book to note Ahasuerus's command to Vashti (1:15) and Mordecai's command to Esther (2:20). Now Esther, finally, is also giving such commands; she has increased in stature to do so. "We have gone from a disobedient queen who is on the receiving end of a command that is not observed, to an obedient queen who is able to issue a command that is observed" (Levenson 1997, 131). The beginning of her leadership of the Jews has now been more fully realized (4:16-17), and just as earlier, Mordecai is still dependent upon Esther's authority to actualize his own needs (8:1-2). Throughout the story, Esther has been an individual with dual alignments, Jewish and Persian, having one foot in each community. As the narrative initially introduced her by means of both of these aspects of her being (2:7), now Esther's dual social standing is again emphasized. Her Jewish aspect comes to the fore, through the reidentification of her father; and her Persian aspect also is evident, as she is referred to thrice as queen in this section. Now, at the conclusion of the story, has Esther finally been able to integrate successfully these two aspects of her social obligations, leader both of the Jews and of the Persians? If so, such integration is another sign of her growing maturity.

The final section of the episode includes two elements, a report about Ahasuerus's actions (10:1) and an exposition about Mordecai's greatness (10:2-3). Most of the content of this brief section is summary; the only new information pertains to Ahasuerus's imposition of tribute on his empire and to Mordecai's inclusion in the royal annals. The reference to "the islands of the sea" is surprising, for up to this point no islands or sea have been mentioned in the numerous references to the territory of the kingdom (10:1). The designation probably refers to the eastern Mediterranean, the far western edge of the Persian Empire. Thus the story ends as it begins, stressing Ahasuerus's large geographical territory (1:1). The Hebrew term *mas*, "forced labor," signifies that what Ahasuerus demands of the inhabitants of the land and the islands is taxation or conscripted service of some type. In the end, not only do the Jews come under the enslavement that Esther postulated (7:4), but all territories are now forced into service for the crown. Affliction now falls upon all people, not only one ethnic group.

The importance and distinction of Mordecai is the focus of 10:2-3, which stresses how high in rank he has become. He has gone from humble origins, sitting at the king's gate day after day, to the highest echelon of power. These verses act like a coda that extends out from the story, bridging between the time of its events and the time of the book's audience (Berlin 2001a, 94-95). The roughly contemporaneous book of Judith concludes in a similar fashion as it reports Judith's sterling reputation in the Jewish community for years to come (Jdt 16:21-25). There is a sense of irony in this final acclamation, in that Mordecai initially refused to honor someone, but he ends up receiving honor instead for himself. The reference to Mordecai's Jewishness ("Mordecai the Jew") is another reminder of how open the Persian government has proved itself to be to non-Persians. Though the narrative notes twice how "great" (the Hebrew term *gādôl*) Mordecai is, it also uses the same word, as a verb, to describe Ahasuerus's action toward him. The phrase in 10:2 reads, literally, "the greatness of Mordecai, whom the king made great." The repetition of this term highlights the fact that Mordecai is not a self-made man but has been given his power by someone else (cf. 8:1-2). Haman was likewise given his position of authority (made "great," 3:1). The reader now understands that the greatness observed at 9:4 was a result of Ahasuerus's actions on Mordecai's behalf; this is how things happen in the palace environment.

The book begins and ends with male aggrandizement, with testimonies to how great certain men are. The story began by emphasizing Ahasuerus's power and wealth (1:1-4), and here it concludes by similarly emphasizing the power of another man, Mordecai (10:1-3). The female characters of the story—Vashti, Zeresh, and Esther—have come and gone between these two bookend attestations to male prestige. At the end of the events Esther finds herself eclipsed. Her role in this episode and in the previous episode has been small in comparison to that of her cousin Mordecai. Initially, Esther had acted as the Jews' commander, telling them what to do (4:16-17). As the story has progressed, however, Mordecai has been increasingly appropriating her role, first by taking it upon himself to write the decree

(8:7-14), and now by doing the greater part in authorizing the Purim festival. Mordecai initiated the predicament for the Jews; Esther did the work and took on the danger to fix the problem. Yet in the end he receives the honor and glory and she remains unacknowledged. Just as Vashti was banished physically, Esther experiences literary banishment as the conclusion of the book focuses solely upon Mordecai. Esther's position in the story reflects the all-too-common experience of real women in patriarchal societies whose hard work goes unacknowledged and unappreciated.

As Mordecai and Esther, in their letter about Purim, wish well-being ("peace"; *šālôm*) to the present Jews, Mordecai correspondingly wishes that same well-being ("welfare"; *šālôm*) to his future generations. The final statement of the book, 10:3*b*, displays fine instances of synonymous parallelism: "he was powerful among the Jews and popular with his many kindred" and "he sought the good of his people and interceded for the welfare of all his descendants." "The Jews" parallels "the people," and "his many kindred" parallels "all his descendants." The first pair represent the entire realm of the Jewish community, the Jewish population as a whole; and the second pair represent familial designations. Mordecai is described, therefore, as having influence both among his relatives and within the Persian Jewish community at large; these parallel terms result in a holistic effect. He is also given an aura of family that he has never had to this point; no wife or children other than his cousin Esther have been indicated. Who are these descendants and (male) kindred?

The narrative raises a rhetorical question about Mordecai's being included in "the annals of the kings of Media and Persia." Though it sounds prestigious to be written up in the official royal annals, one must remember what dull documents they actually are (6:1). As no intimation of their importance is suggested in the environment of this story, the reader wonders whether anyone who wishes to stay awake ever consults them! This final statement about Mordecai's greatness notes that he is second in rank to the king, but then lists his influence only among the Jews. Does this observation suggest that he does not have similar influence upon the rest of the people, the non-Jews, in the Persian kingdom? Or, as "Mordecai the Jew," perhaps he continues to feel that his primary loyalty should remain with the Jews. At its conclusion, therefore, the story maintains its continued concern with the Jewish community.

Theological and Ethical Analysis

The overriding focus of this final episode is upon remembrance. Acts of commemoration serve to enhance the communal memory, the memory of a people. In essence, such remembrance forges and solidifies identity; it functions to answer the question, "Who are we as a people?" Again and again throughout the episode, the Jews are told to commemorate the event of their victory. The holiday of Purim, therefore, represents a time placed into the liturgical year specifically for remembrance. Such recollection also leads to understanding. Just as the yearly celebration of Independence Day functions both to remind one of an event in the past and also to teach one what it is to be a citizen of the United States, so the yearly celebration of Purim reminds and teaches what it is to be a Jew and a member of the Jewish community. The prescribed remembering is not merely a mental activity but also a physical one; commemoration is accomplished through the performance of specified actions. The story, therefore, demonstrates a concern for tradition, for teaching to the next generation and then to subsequent generations, and in this way the story will never be lost. Continuance and comprehensiveness are of utmost importance. Purim, the commemoration of the Jews' salvation, is to be done by every single generation, every single year, by every single family, in every single place. Tradition could not be deemed more central.

This final portion of the book displays correspondence with some of the concerns of the book of Deuteronomy. In Deuteronomy, also, the community's current action is to be based on past events in Israelite history: it is essential for the people to remember. In addition to memory, the story's themes of instruction to descendants and concern for the poor also reflect emphases throughout Deuteronomy (e.g., Deut 4:9; 6:7; 8:11-20; 24:10-22). Yet even the concept of remembering serves to show the secular overtone of the book of

Esther. In Deuteronomy, the community is instructed to remember *YHWH* and what YHWH had done for the Israelites in the past. In the book of Esther, the Jews are instead instructed to remember what *people* (their ancestors) had done to bring about their own victory.

A new model of leadership is presented, one that is more collaborative and less hierarchical. In the process of establishing Purim, the Jews enact a different type of leadership than that of the Persian administration. It is not a top-down model, with all authority lying in the hand of the king, but a more democratic process. Esther and Mordecai merely make official that which the people, the Jews themselves, have already begun to do (Fox 2001, 227-28). In the language of modern religious experience, one would say that this final scene emphasizes the significance of the laity, rather than of clergy, to initiate change. A good leader often needs to follow the direction of the people. Moreover, it is significant that the instruction about what the Jews are to do in celebrating Purim does not come from a high religious authority (the high priest, for instance), but instead from a high *political* authority. One would not necessarily expect that Mordecai, a common Jew, would be given sanction to dictate a new religious festival. This detail is a further signal of how the Jews in the book of Esther look not to the temple but to the state for their direction.

The reference to fasting and lamenting is not to be glossed over. Esther's command that the remembrance of these events also include lamentation serves as a check for the Jews, present and future. This letter follows all the celebrating throughout chapters 8–10, after much rejoicing and happiness. But even such a brief mention of lamentation suggests that the Jews, as a people, will not always be in a place of such gladness, that they will again feel sorrow and sadness. Life will never be all joy and parties. Esther's injunction hints that this will not be the last instance of genocide for the Jews, that throughout the generations there will always be Hamans around who wish ill on the Jews. Her instructions to weep as well as to laugh, to mourn as well as to dance, recognize that life is lived between joy and sorrow.

In such dark times the celebration of Purim becomes especially important. Purim is a frivolous event, filled with banqueting, costumes, cheering, noisemaking, laughter, playacting, drunkenness, and gifts—the story's carnivalesque atmosphere actualized in real experience. The "psychological release" that this holiday brings is why it is essential to continue to observe it year after year (Berlin 2001a, xlv-xlix). Properly celebrating Purim in the prescribed fashion during times of despair and oppression, in essence, forces one to be happy for a day; this reenactment of the original Jews' experience causes later communities to remember the sense of freedom and reminds them that someday there will again be joyous times.

Of no lesser importance is the injunction to give gifts. Mordecai's instructions legislate generosity; the celebration of Purim would not be complete without looking outside oneself, without considering those who are less fortunate. A modern Jewish theologian argues that, in ghettos and concentration camps during the Shoah, there was great significance in the small acts of kindness that women performed for one another—the sharing of a morsel of food, the cutting off half of one's blanket to give away, the washing of another's sores. If God was to be found anywhere in the Shoah, it was in such actions of one person toward another (Raphael 2003). It may be, therefore, that the only way to make meaning out of devastation and destruction, oppression and bloodshed, is to focus on the small kindnesses, the small acts of grace, that still persist; when there seems to be nothing redemptive in the irrational hatred of Haman and his successors, to look to the actions of ordinary people. Perhaps if we are looking for God only in grand victories, we are looking for the wrong kind of God. Perhaps if a divine presence is to be found anywhere in the Esther tradition, it lies in such small generosities of average people, generation after generation, giving gifts of food to those who are hungry.

The book of Esther concludes on a note of hope and optimism. The final verses describe how Mordecai is a powerful and popular leader. Surely, now that Mordecai is in charge, things in the Persian kingdom will get better. It is, though, an open-ended statement; there is the sense that the story continues on, that Mordecai's influence will endure past his term in office. The conclusion, therefore, conveys a sense of satisfaction and completion. The very fact of Mordecai's victory and prominence guarantees the Jewish community that it will continue long into the future. This forward-looking conclusion represents the hope that all parents have for their children, that the next generation will have an easier life and not have to endure the same troubles. To have a Jew in such a top-ranking official position indicates that the Jews will always have someone in high places looking out for their interests, interceding for their welfare. More broadly, it suggests that governments will always include a "Mordecai," a watchdog who looks out for human rights violations. If not him, then someone will arise "from another quarter" to work against oppression, to assure that justice is done. The book concludes with a sense of optimism that, in the future, political administrations will be more careful to counter injustice and discrimination against any of their peoples. We are left with the hope that such evil will never again be allowed to flourish.

SELECT BIBLIOGRAPHY

WORKS CITED

Albright, William F. 1974. "The Lachish Cosmetic Burner and Esther 2:12." In *A Light Unto My Path: Old Testament Studies in Honor of Jacob M. Myers*. Edited by Howard N. Bream, Ralph D. Heim, and Carey A. Moore, 25-32. Philadelphia: Temple University Press.

Bach, Alice. 1997. *Women, Seduction, and Betrayal in Biblical Narrative*. Cambridge: Cambridge University Press.

Bal, Mieke. 1991. "Lots of Writing." *Semeia* 54:77-102.

Bankson, Marjory Zoet. 1985. *Braided Streams: Esther and a Woman's Way of Growing*. San Diego: LuraMedia.

Beller, David. 1997. "A Theology of the Book of Esther." *Restoration Quarterly* 39:1-15.

Berg, Sandra Beth. 1980. "After the Exile: God and History in the Books of Chronicles and Esther." In *The Divine Helmsman: Studies on God's Control of Human Events, Presented to Lou H. Silberman*. Edited by James L. Crenshaw and Samuel Sandmel, 107-27. New York: Ktav.

Bergey, Ronald L. 1984. "Late Linguistic Features in Esther." *Jewish Quarterly Review* LXXV:66-78.

———. 1988. "Post-Exilic Hebrew Linguistic Developments in Esther: A Diachronic Approach." *Journal of the Evangelical Theological Society* 31:161-68.

Berkovits, Eliezer. 1973. *Faith After the Holocaust*. New York: Ktav.

Berlin, Adele. 2001b. "The Book of Esther and Ancient Storytelling." *Journal of Biblical Literature* 120:3-14.

Berman, Joshua. 2001. "*Hadassah Bat Abihail*: The Evolution from Object to Subject in the Character of Esther." *Journal of Biblical Literature* 120:647-69.

Besser, Saul P. 1969. "Esther and Purim—Chance and Play." *Central Conference of American Rabbis Journal* 16:36-42.

Brenner, Athalya. 1994. "Who's Afraid of Feminist Criticism? Who's Afraid of Biblical Humour? The Case of the Obtuse Foreign Ruler in the Hebrew Bible." *Journal for the Study of the Old Testament* 63:38-55.

———. 1995. "Looking at Esther Through the Looking Glass." In *A Feminist Companion to Esther, Judith, and Susanna*. Edited by Athalya Brenner, 71-80. The Feminist Companion to the Bible 7. Sheffield: Sheffield Academic Press.

Bronner, Leila L. 1998. "Reclaiming Esther: From Sex Object to Sage." *The Jewish Bible Quarterly* XXVI:3-11.

Clines, David J. A. 1984b. *Ezra, Nehemiah, Esther*. New Century Bible Commentary. Grand Rapids: Eerdmans.

———. 1990. "Reading Esther from Left to Right: Contemporary Strategies for Reading a Biblical Text." In *The Bible in Three Dimensions: Essays in Celebration of Forty Years of Biblical Studies in the University of Sheffield*. Edited by David J. A. Clines, Stephen E. Fowl, and Stanley Porter, 31-52. Journal for the Study of the Old Testament Supplement Series 87. Sheffield: Sheffield Academic Press.

Cole, Susan Guettel. 1981. "Could Greek Women Read and Write?" In *Reflections of Women in Antiquity*. Edited by Helene P. Foley, 219-45. New York: Gorden and Breach Science Publishers.

Comstock, Gary David. 1993. *Gay Theology Without Apology*. Cleveland: Pilgrim Press.

Costas, Orlando E. 1988. "The Subversiveness of Faith: Esther as a Paradigm for a Liberating Theology." *The Ecumenical Review* 40:66-78.

Craghan, John F. 1986. "Esther: A Fully Liberated Woman." *The Bible Today* 24:6-11.

Crawford, Sidnie White. 1996. "Has Every Book of the Bible Been Found Among the Dead Sea Scrolls?" *Bible Review* XII:28-33, 56.

Crenshaw, James L. 1998. *Education in Ancient Israel: Across the Deadening Silence*. The Anchor Bible Reference Library. New York: Doubleday.

Day, Linda. 1995. *Three Faces of a Queen: Characterization in the Books of Esther*. Journal for the Study of the Old Testament Supplement Series 186. Sheffield: Sheffield Academic Press.

———. 1998. "Power, Otherness, and Gender in the Biblical Short Stories." *Horizons in Biblical Theology: An International Dialogue* 20:109-27.

De Troyer, Kristin. 2000. *The End of the Alpha Text of Esther: Translation and Narrative Technique in MT 8:1-17, LXX 8:1-17, and AT 7:14-41*. Society of Biblical Literature Septuagint and Cognate Studies Series 48. Atlanta: Society of Biblical Literature.

Dorothy, Charles V. 1997. *The Books of Esther: Structure, Genre, and Textual Integrity.* Journal for the Study of the Old Testament Supplement Series 189. Sheffield: Sheffield Academic Press.

Edwards, Russel K. 1990. "Reply to 'Ahasuerus is the Villain.'" *Jewish Bible Quarterly* 19:34-39.

Fackenheim, Emil L. 1990. *The Jewish Bible After the Holocaust: A Rereading.* Bloomington: Indiana University Press.

Fewell, Danna Nolan. 1992. "Introduction: Writing, Reading, and Relating." In *Reading Between Texts: Intertextuality and the Hebrew Bible.* Edited by Danna Nolan Fewell, 11-20. Literary Currents in Biblical Interpretation. Louisville: Westminster John Knox Press.

Fried, Lisbeth S. 2000. "Towards the *Ur*-Text of Esther." *Journal for the Study of the Old Testament* 88:49-57.

Fuchs, Esther. 1982. "Status and Role of Female Heroines in the Biblical Narrative." *Mankind Quarterly* 23:149-60.

Gendler, Mary. 1976. "The Restoration of Vashti." In *The Jewish Woman: New Perspectives.* Edited by Elizabeth Koltun, 241-47. New York: Schocken.

Goldman, Stan. 1990. "Narrative and Ethical Ironies in Esther." *Journal for the Study of the Old Testament* 47:15-31.

Greenstein, Edward L. 1987. "A Jewish Reading of Esther." In *Judaic Perspectives on Ancient Israel.* Edited by Jacob Neusner, Baruch A. Levine, and Ernst S. Frerichs, 225-43. Philadelphia: Fortress Press.

Hallo, William W. 1983. "The First Purim." *Biblical Archaeologist* 46:19-26.

Horbury, William. 1991. "The Name Mardochaeus in a Ptolemaic Inscription." *Vetus Testamentum* XLI:220-26.

Horn, Siegfried H. 1964. "Mordecai, a Historical Problem." *Biblical Research* 9:14-25.

Humphreys, W. Lee. 1973. "A Life-Style for Diaspora: A Study of the Tales of Esther and Daniel." *Journal for Biblical Literature* 92:211-23.

———. 1985. "The Story of Esther and Mordecai: An Early Jewish Novella." In *Saga, Legend, Tale, Novella, Fable: Narrative Forms in Old Testament Literature.* Edited by George W. Coats, 97-113. Journal for the Study of the Old Testament Supplement Series 35. Sheffield: JSOT Press.

Ilan, Tal. 1995. *Jewish Women in Greco-Roman Palestine: An Inquiry into Image and Status.* Texte und Studien zum antiken Judentum 44. Tübingen: Mohr.

———. 1999. *Integrating Women into Second Temple History.* Texte und Studien zum antiken Judentum 76. Tübingen: Mohr Siebeck.

Jobes, Karen H. 1996. *The Alpha-Text of Esther: Its Character and Relationship to the Masoretic Text.* Society of Biblical Literature Dissertation Series 153. Atlanta: Scholars Press.

Jones, Bruce William. 1977. "Two Misconceptions About the Book of Esther." *Catholic Biblical Quarterly* 39:171-81.

————. 1978. "The So-Called Appendix to the Book of Esther." *Semitics* 6:36-43.

Kirk-Duggan, Cheryl A. 1999. "Black Mother Women and Daughters: Signifying Female-Divine Relationships in the Hebrew Bible and African-American Mother-Daughter Short Stories." In *Ruth and Esther: A Feminist Companion to the Bible (Second Series).* Edited by Athalya Brenner, 192-210. The Feminist Companion to the Bible (Second Series) 3. Sheffield: Sheffield Academic Press.

Klein, Lillian R. 1995. "Honor and Shame in Esther." In *A Feminist Companion to Esther, Judith, and Susanna.* Edited by Athalya Brenner, 149-75. The Feminist Companion to the Bible 7. Sheffield: Sheffield Academic Press.

LaCocque, André. 1987. "Haman in the Book of Esther." *Hebrew Annual Review* 11:207-17.

Laffey, Alice L. 1998. *An Introduction to the Old Testament: A Feminist Perspective.* Philadelphia: Fortress Press.

Loewenstamm, Samuel E. 1971. "Esther 9:29-32: The Genesis of a Late Addition." *Hebrew Union College Annual* 42:117-24.

McKane, W. 1961. "A Note on Esther IX and 1 Samuel XV." *Journal of Theological Studies* 12:260-61.

Moore, Carey A. 1977. *Daniel, Esther, and Jeremiah: The Additions.* The Anchor Bible 44. Garden City: Doubleday.

————, ed. 1982. *Studies in the Book of Esther.* New York: Ktav.

Mosala, Itumeleng J. 1992. "The Implications of the Text of Esther for African Women's Struggle for Liberation in South Africa." *Semeia* 59:129-37.

Niditch, Susan. 1987. *Underdogs and Tricksters: A Prelude to Biblical Folklore.* San Francisco: Harper and Row.

————. 1995. "Short Stories: The Book of Esther and the Theme of Woman as a Civilizing Force." In *Old Testament Interpretation: Past, Present, and Future: Essays in Honor of Gene M. Tucker.* Edited by James Luther Mays, David L. Petersen, and Kent Harold Richards, 195-209. Nashville: Abingdon Press.

Noss, Philip A. 1993. "A Footnote on Time: The Book of Esther." *The Bible Translator* 44:309-20.

Paton, Lewis Bayles. 1908. *A Critical and Exegetical Commentary on the Book of Esther.* The International Critical Commentary. New York: Scribner's.

Polish, Daniel F. 1999. "Aspects of Esther: A Phenomenological Exploration of the *Megillah* of Esther and the Origins of Purim." *Journal for the Study of the Old Testament* 85:85-106.

Radday, Yehuda T. 1990. "Esther with Humour." In *On Humour and the Comic in the Hebrew Bible.* Edited by Yehuda T. Radday and Athalya Brenner, 295-313. Bible and Literature Series 23. Sheffield: Almond.

Raphael, Melissa. 2003. *The Female Face of God in Auschwitz: A Jewish Feminist Theology of the Holocaust.* Religion and Gender. New York: Routledge.

Salvesen, Alison. 1999. "כֶתֶר (Esther 1:11; 2:17; 6:8): Something to Do with a Camel?" *Journal of Semitic Studies* XLIV: 35-46.

Sedgwick, Eve Kosofsky. 1990. *Epistemology of the Closet.* Berkeley: University of California Press.

Segal, Eliezer. 1989. "Human Anger and Divine Intervention in Esther." *Prooftexts* 9:247-56.

Sweeney, Marvin A. 1998. "Reconceiving the Paradigms of Old Testament Theology in the Post-*Shoah* Period." *Biblical Interpretation* VI:142-61.

Talmon, Shemaryahu. 1963. "'Wisdom' in the Book of Esther." *Vetus Testamentum* 13:419-55.

———. 1995. "Was the Book of Esther Known at Qumran?" *Dead Sea Discoveries: A Journal of Current Research on the Scrolls and Related Literature* II:249-67.

Torrey, Charles C. 1944. "The Older Book of Esther." *Harvard Theological Review* 37:1-40.

van Wijk-Bos, Johanna W. H. 1998. *Ezra, Nehemiah, and Esther.* Westminster Bible Companion. Louisville: Westminster John Knox Press.

Walsh, Carey Ellen. 2000. "Under the Influence: Trust and Risk in Biblical Family Drinking." *Journal for the Study of the Old Testament* 90:13-29.

White, Sidnie Ann. 1989. "Esther: A Feminist Model for Jewish Diaspora." In *Gender and Difference in Ancient Israel.* Edited by Peggy L. Day, 161-77. Minneapolis: Fortress Press.

Wills, Lawrence M. 1990. *The Jew in the Court of the Foreign King: Ancient Jewish Court Legends.* Harvard Dissertations in Religion 26. Minneapolis: Fortress Press.

———. 1995. *The Jewish Novel in the Ancient World.* Myth and Poetics. Ithaca: Cornell University Press.

Wyler, Bea. 1995. "Esther: The Incomplete Emancipation of a Queen."

In *A Feminist Companion to Esther, Judith, and Susanna.* Edited by Athalya Brenner, 111-35. The Feminist Companion to the Bible 7. Sheffield: Sheffield Academic Press.

Yamauchi, Edwin M. 1992. "Mordecai, the Persepolis Tablets, and the Susa Excavations." *Vetus Testamentum* XLII:272-75.

COMMENTARIES

Beal, Timothy K. 1999. *Esther.* In *Ruth and Esther.* Edited by David W. Colter. Berit Olam. Collegeville: The Liturgical Press.—Creative interpretation of the book of Esther, with focus upon literary and methodological concerns.

Bechtel, Carol M. 2002. *Esther.* Interpretation. Louisville: John Knox Press.—A treatment of the book of Esther, with attention to theological concerns, for a more generalist audience. Includes comments on the Greek Additions.

Berlin, Adele. 2001a. *Esther.* The JPS Bible Commentary. Philadelphia: The Jewish Publication Society.—Emphasizes the comedic character of the book of Esther and reads it in light of contemporaneous Greek historiography and midrashic interpretation.

Bush, Frederic W. 1996. *Esther.* In *Ruth, Esther.* Word Biblical Commentary 9. Dallas: Word Publishing.—A detailed and thorough commentary with various charts delineating the book's structure. Includes philological notes and extensive bibliography.

Crawford, Sidnie White. 1999. *The Book of Esther* and *The Additions to Esther.* In *The New Interpreter's Bible* III, 853-972. Nashville: Abingdon Press.—Even-handed commentary on the Hebrew book and the Greek Additions, including discussion of the questions of the book of Esther at Qumran and theological reflections.

Levenson, Jon D. 1997. *Esther: A Commentary.* The Old Testament Library. Louisville: Westminster John Knox Press.—A brief commentary whose strength lies in its suggestions about the structure of the book of Esther. Attempts a compromise story by integrating the Greek Additions into the Hebrew version.

Moore, Carey A. 1971. *Esther: Introduction, Translation, and Notes.* The Anchor Bible 7B. Garden City: Doubleday.—Authored by a scholar who dedicated much of his academic career to the book of Esther, this work served as the major modern English commentary for years. Special attention given to the concerns of canonicity and historiography.

SELECTED STUDIES

Beal, Timothy K. 1997. *The Book of Hiding: Gender, Ethnicity, Annihilation, and Esther.* Biblical Limits. New York: Routledge.— This work draws aspects of the book of Esther into conversation with postmodern theorists, with particular attention upon the instabilities of gender and ethnic identities it presents.

Berg, Sandra Beth. 1979. *The Book of Esther: Motifs, Themes, and Structure.* Society of Biblical Literature Dissertation Series 44. Missoula: Scholars Press.—An assessment of certain of the major themes (banquets, kingship, obedience, power, loyalty, reversal) of the book of Esther and a comparison of it with the Joseph story.

Clines, David J. A. 1984a. *The Esther Scroll: The Story of the Story.* Journal for the Study of the Old Testament Supplement Series 30. Sheffield: JSOT Press.—A forerunner of recent concerns about the textual history of the book of Esther and the relationships among its three primary versions, with a proposed delineation of five developmental layers of the story. Includes an English translation of the Greek A (Alpha) Text.

Craig, Kenneth M. 1995. *Reading Esther: A Case for the Literary Carnivalesque.* Literary Currents in Biblical Interpretation. Louisville: Westminster John Knox Press.—Assessment of the book of Esther as an example of the genre of carnivalesque, as explicated in the scholarship of literary theorist Mikhail Bakhtin.

Fox, Michael V. 1991. *The Redaction of the Books of Esther: On Reading Composite Texts.* The Society of Biblical Literature Monograph Series 40. Atlanta: Scholars Press.—A detailed proposal of the redactional processes and objectives in the production of the Massoretic Text and the A Text versions of the book of Esther, including thoughts on the methodology of redaction criticism in general.

———. 2001. *Character and Ideology in the Book of Esther.* Second Edition. Grand Rapids: Eerdmans.—A hybrid endeavor, including both standard commentary and thorough analysis of each of the primary characters in the story.

Laniak, Timothy S. 1998. *Shame and Honor in the Book of Esther.* Society of Biblical Literature Dissertation Series 165. Atlanta: Scholars Press.—Consideration of the book of Esther in light of the sociological categories of honor and shame, both individual and national.